THE
OTHELLO
RESPONSE

THE OTHELLO RESPONSE

Conquering Jealousy, Betrayal and Rage
in Your Relationship

DR. KENNETH C. RUGE
AND
BARRY LENSON

MARLOWE & COMPANY
NEW YORK

THE OTHELLO RESPONSE: *Conquering Jealousy, Betrayal and Rage in Your Relationship*
Copyright © 2003 by Dr. Kenneth C. Ruge and Barry Lenson

Published by
Marlowe & Company
An Imprint of Avalon Publishing Group Incorporated
245 West 17th Street, 11th Floor
New York, NY 10011

Grateful acknowledgment is made to the following for permission to reprint previously published material:
Quotation from *Raging Bull* on p. 56: copyright © 1980 Metro-Goldwyn-Mayer Studios Inc. All Rights Reserved.

Library of Congress Cataloging-in-Publication Data
Ruge, Kenneth.
    The Othello response: conquering jealousy, betrayal and rage in
  your relationship / Kenneth C. Ruge ; with Barry Lenson.
      p. cm.
    Includes bibliographical references and index.
    ISBN 1-56924-503-7
    1. Jealousy. I. Lenson, Barry. II. Title.

  BF575.J4R84 2003
  152.4'8–dc21

9 8 7 6 5 4 3 2 1

Designed by Simon M. Sullivan
Printed in the United States of America
Distributed by Publishers Group West

For our parents
who did their best to live kindly, love us, and be gentle to each other
despite the many challenges life placed in their paths

O, beware, my lord, of jealousy;
It is the green-eyed monster which doth mock
The meat it feeds on . . .
　　　　　—Iago, in *Othello*

CONTENTS

INTRODUCTION
CONFRONTING THE GREEN-EYED MONSTER

EVEN THOUGH WE MAY be enlightened modern people, jealousy has not left our side. The newspapers we read daily, the news programs we watch at night, the afternoon talk shows that tempt us: all these deliver steady doses of news about modern people who do horrible things after giving in to violent jealousy.

In the pages ahead, we will discover many such stories. For now, let's just look at one pulled at random from recent stories in the news.

She just had this evil look on her face . . . she said she could kill my father for what he'd done to her . . . She stomped on the accelerator and went for him. He was really scared, I know that he was trying to get away and he couldn't. I felt the bumps . . . She wasn't sorry. She had killed him.

Those are the words of Lindsey Harris, a high school student from Columbus, Ohio, as she testified on January 29, 2003, at the Houston murder trial of her stepmother, Clara Harris. Clara Harris, forty-four, was on trial for the murder of her husband, Dr. David Harris, a dentist who had been having an affair with a Gail Bridges, thirty-eight, who worked in his office.

Lindsey Harris was in Clara Harris's car at the time of her father's death. She witnessed firsthand the devastating power that obsessive jealousy can have. A few days later, Clara Harris was convicted of murder and went to jail.

Of course, we don't all murder people when we become jealous. How much damage can obsessive jealousy cause us when it does not lead up to assault or murder? A great deal more than most of us suspect. Jealousy, even when it works silently beneath the surface, has the potential to rob the joy from our love and our lives.

Consider just a few tales of jealousy we discovered as we researched and wrote this book:

■ We met men and women whose marriages and loving relationships had become virtual prisons due to constant fear of jealous outbursts from their partners. Often, these victims had decided to simply live with the problem instead of confronting it. That was often an unwise choice that only delayed the onset of psychological and physical abuse.

■ We talked with men and women who did not own up to being obsessively jealous, but who refused to allow their spouses or partners to take jobs or attend social events outside the home. They had devised elaborate ways to "conceal" their partners at home where they could not be noticed by other potential partners. And for their partners and themselves, life had become excruciating.

■ We discovered men and women who tried to destroy the self-esteem of their partners so that they would feel too ugly or unsuccessful to attract rival suitors. Many of the partners were highly attractive, intelligent men and women who had actually come to believe they were failures, unworthy of notice. They were the "other" victims of jealousy: crippled, unable to move ahead in their lives. Often, they did not even realize their partner's jealousy was at the root of their ills.

■ We spoke with men and women who said that their partners or spouses were cold and unfeeling at home. Yet these same "cold" individuals often engaged in extravagant acts of affection in public to demonstrate dominance. The "victims" of these odd behaviors, again, often did not recognize that jealousy was at the root of their problems.

Sometimes, such patterns become so ingrained in the fabric of relationships that people do not fully comprehend the damage that is occurring.

Perhaps most troubling of all are the stories of the children who get swept up in the jealous tide, children who

■ Have mothers or fathers who are the victims of domestic violence.

■ Are themselves the victims of an abusive parent's jealous rage.

■ Have a parent who unbalances the family with the subtle plots, manipulations, and intrigues that spring from veiled jealousy.

- Learn patterns of jealousy and unfaithfulness from their parents that they will replicate in their own adult years.

WHY WE WROTE THIS BOOK AND WHY YOU SHOULD READ IT

The victims of this epidemic—and *epidemic* is not too strong a word—need help. To date, no other book has stepped up to the challenge and addressed obsessional jealousy head-on. There are books about men and anger, about divorce, about personal recovery and discovery. But no book has appeared that deals with a syndrome that is so widespread, we have given it a new name: the Othello response.

We know that when we name a problem, we can gain some power over it.

Why should you read this book? What help and advice will you receive? We tried to keep those questions squarely in our crosshairs as we researched, planned, and wrote this book. We knew that if we failed to stay centered on helping our readers by addressing those issues, this book would become, at best, a collection of interesting essays that would not make a difference in people's lives.

These are the benefits we believe this book can provide:

- *If you are not sure whether difficulties you are experiencing in your love relationship are tied to jealousy,* you will learn to recognize whether it is affecting you or your partner. Unless the problem is brought into the light of day and its presence understood, it will almost certainly continue to do damage. Looking the other way will not help.

- *If you already know you suffer from obsessive-compulsive jealousy* or if your partner does, this book can bring you the help you need to begin to correct the problem and, ultimately, break free of its hold. You will learn healthy, practical steps that will prevent further damage and heal any damage that has occurred so far.

■ *If you discover that the Othello response* is not at work in your relationship but want to prevent it, you will discover ways to keep it from "infecting" you. In effect, you will insulate your relationship from jealousy and prevent the Othello response from taking over.

■ *If you are trying to heal your relationship* in the wake of an actual affair or infidelity, you will discover the essential tools and skills you need to hasten the healing process and rebuild goodwill. Of if you have had a previous love relationship destroyed by the Othello response, you will gain insights on preventing it from happening again.

■ *If you are recovering alone from an infidelity that ended your last relationship,* you will learn outlooks and skills you need to ensure greater happiness and satisfaction in future relationships. There is no need to move from one relationship to another, only to run into the same problems again.

THE DEEPER REWARDS OF UNDERSTANDING JEALOUSY

Finally, it is our hope that, through this book, you will learn to honor and strengthen your love relationship and be more successful in it. As we have written this book, we have gained a great deal of respect for the force of jealousy, the kind of respect we accord to a dangerous and wily adversary.

We have also encountered several remarkable truths about

jealousy that we would like you to discover too. They are at the heart of this book, and there is no point in holding them back until the later chapters.

First, remaining grounded in reality of your relationship is the greatest, most practical antidote and cure against the Othello response. If we consider the play *Othello* for a moment, we see that if Othello had taken only a few moments to gather accurate information about what was really taking place in his wife's world, his jealous imaginings would have vanished like a light haze. Yet Othello never does that. He never takes the most obvious steps to alleviate his jealous agony. He just gives in. He never investigates. He never asks the right questions. He never talks to Desdemona, his wife, to get a reality-based glimpse into her life and her world. Instead, he allows himself to be seduced by a false reality (a sort of jealous Othello "trance") that Iago weaves for him, and which he creates even more compellingly for himself.

Second, protectiveness and jealousy, if understood and respected, can strengthen and deepen our love relationships. If understood and kept in check, jealousy offers a profound compliment to our partners. It honors them. It tells them that we are deeply complimented that they have chosen us over the many other partners who might have been available to them.

If respected and understood, jealousy can enhance the richness, the sense of value, and even the intimacy of our love. But to stand in the bright light of that day, we first need to chase the dark clouds away. To do that, we need to appreciate the formidable power that jealousy has to unsettle our lives. And that requires understanding.

PART ONE
THE OTHELLO RESPONSE
UNMASKED

What is the Othello response? When and how does it start? How does it progress? What damage can it cause in our relationships and our lives? And are we all liable to be hurt by it?

We need to consider those questions carefully. Only then can we set about the hard work of preventing the damage that the Othello response can cause in our lives.

CHAPTER 1

THE OTHELLO RESPONSE:
ANATOMY OF AN EPIDEMIC

Iago: Do it not with poison, strangle her in her bed, even the bed
she hath contaminated.

Othello: Good, good: the justice of it pleases: very good.

—Iago counsels Othello on how to murder Desdemona.

Othello, Act IV, Scene 1

SHAKESPEARE'S PLAY *Othello* TELLS the story of a newly married, loving husband named Othello who kills Desdemona, his innocent wife, after a soldier named Iago persuades him that she is having sex with another man. Othello then kills himself. Along the way, he brings death and injury to a number of other people. Since the tragedy was first performed four hundred years ago, *Othello* has come to be regarded as a masterpiece of theater, literature, and insight into human nature.

"TO DIE UPON A KISS"

In *Othello,* Shakespeare created a perfect model of the Othello response in all its power and complexity. How was he able to so accurately reproduce the chain of psychological events that is triggered from the moment we begin to doubt our lovers?

Perhaps most important of all, what can Shakespeare teach us that helps us understand ourselves better and prevent the Othello response from taking hold in our lives?

The first step is to take a close look and understand the play better.

THE PLOT

Shakespeare's play is set in medieval times in two locales: Venice and the island of Cyprus. Othello, a Moorish mercenary sea captain, has been employed by the Duke of Venice to oversee naval operations in a war against the Turks.

Before the play begins, two significant events have taken place:

- Othello has promoted a capable soldier named Cassio to the rank of lieutenant, bypassing another career soldier named Iago who was seeking the same position. Iago now despises Othello and plans revenge against him. Yet as the play begins, Iago has no definite plans in place about how he will bring bring Othello to ruin. He is simply resolved to harm him.

- Othello has just eloped with Desdemona, the young daughter of a prominent Venetian citizen named Brabantio.

Through the play, Iago brilliantly exacts his vengeance and destroys Othello and his new bride. Manipulating happenstance events and false evidence, Iago quickly convinces Othello that his new wife is having a sexual relationship with Cassio, who is in reality a respectful and honorable man. Othello is so completely taken in by Iago's lies that he is driven wild with jealousy. Finally he strangles Desdemona in her bed. Only after this horrific deed is done does he realize Iago tricked him. In an instant, he sees the truth and the falsehood of Iago.

Yet in his deepest self, didn't Othello know the truth all along, that his wife was innocent? We believe he did, but he became addicted to a false, alternative reality that drove him to violence.

But what does *Othello* have to do with us today? Few of us are like the play's central character, a Moorish naval captain named Othello employed as a mercenary in medieval Venice. We are modern, enlightened people. When we encounter problems in our loving relationships, we listen, we think, and we communicate. We don't kill people, especially not the people we love. We work things out.

Or do we? If we are so modern, why are the cruel truths of *Othello* always with us? Up-to-date though we may be, the stubborn realities of jealousy and retribution will not go away. With variations, we hear *Othello's* story most nights on the evening news. Nearly every time we open a newspaper, we find stories of jealousy, betrayal, rage, and revenge.

The statistics tell us that jealousy-related violence remains a problem of epidemic proportions. It is the leading cause of murder in the world and the most common reason for domestic violence and spouse abuse. It is also one of the most common reasons for divorce, more prevalent than we realize because jealousy tends to be underreported when statistics are compiled. It is a major contributing cause of brutality against children, stalking of former lovers, and other harrowing realities of modern life.

STATISTICS FROM THE U.S. BUREAU OF JUSTICE

How prevalent are the violent outcomes that accompany obsessive jealousy? Although it is a problem worldwide, let us consider these statistics about violent crime in the United States alone, compiled by the government's Bureau of Justice:

- Between 1976 and 2000, 512,599 people were murdered in the United States.

- Of them, 14 percent did not know their assailants. However, 11 percent of them not only knew their assailants, they were killed by an "intimate"—meaning a current or former spouse or lover. And 7.1 percent were killed by a current spouse.

■ In all, 4.3 percent of all murdered people were killed by a boyfriend or girlfriend.

■ A total of 33.3 percent of all female murder victims were killed by an intimate, compared to 4 percent of all male murder victims.

■ Of all children under age five murdered between 1976 and 2000, 31 percent were killed by fathers, 30 percent were killed by mothers, 23 percent were killed by male acquaintances, 7 percent were killed by other relatives — and only 3 percent were killed by strangers. Of those killed by someone other than a parent, 82 percent were killed by males. Although no statistics have been compiled about the role of jealousy in these murders, it is assumed to be a leading factor. When the people take revenge against their current or former lovers or spouses, children are often the victims.

■ In general, guns are most often used in intimate homicide but weapon type varies by relationship. Between 1990 and 2000, more than two-thirds of spouse and ex-spouse victims were killed with guns. When killed by intimates, men and boyfriends are more likely to be killed by knives.

JEALOUSY AND MURDER

Studies from around the globe confirm that male sexual jealousy is the leading cause of murders in the world — possibly at the root of 50 percent of the world's homicides. Sexual jealousy is often the reason why women murder men. But in many cases, women murder in order to protect themselves from husbands or lovers who have become jealous and violent.

Of course, murder is not the only criminal activity that results from the Othello response. Spousal beatings, child abuse, assaults, stalking, and damage to property are only a few of the things that result when jealousy infects people's hearts and minds.

Again, let's review a sampling of Bureau of Justice statistics:

- Intimate violence is primarily a crime against women. In 1998, females were the victims in 85 percent of nonlethal intimate violence.

- In 2001 alone, women experienced an estimated 588,490 rapes, sexual assaults, robberies, aggravated assaults, and simple assaults at the hands of intimates.

- In 2001, only about 103,220 men were victims of violent crimes by intimates.

- Women between the ages of sixteen and twenty-four experience the highest per capita rates of intimate violence — 19.6 victimizations per every 1,000 women.

- Intimates were identified by female victims as the perpetrators of about 1 percent of all workplace violent crime.

- Stalking is at epidemic proportions. In fact, 12 percent of all women have been stalked at some point in their lives, with former husbands or male lovers the most common perpetrators.

If you spend a few minutes searching in your local library or on the Internet, you can easily turn up many more troubling statistics. They are very easy to come by. Whatever country you live in (be it in the Americas, or Europe, or Asia), obsessive jealousy remains the primary reason people do harm to themselves, to the people they now or once loved, and to children. And often to other people who are unlucky enough to get in the way.

WHO ARE THE PERPETRATORS?

Although men have traditionally been the leading perpetrators of violent acts, jealousy-related violence is becoming less and less of a "male" problem today. More women are joining the ranks of men in committing violent acts as outcomes of jealousy. Nor is jealous violence a "straight" phenomenon. Although research into jealousy-related violence in homosexual and lesbian populations is harder to find than are studies conducted in heterosexual populations, more data is coming in, indicating that violent jealousy is also an acute problem in same-sex partnerships.

The violent outcomes of jealousy are a social problem too. Violently jealous men and women clog our courts and add significantly to our swelling prison population. The victims of jealous rage (the battered and stalked, the children in need of foster care) demand protection in specialized programs and homes.

CASE STUDY: O.J., A NATIONAL MANIA

Who could possibly think that jealousy has exited entirely the stage of modern life when we recall how the trial of O.J. Simpson, that "trial of the century," became a national obsession? In living rooms, offices, and social gatherings from coast to coast, people wanted to know what had really happened. Even if they did not want to know the grim truth, they became obsessed with just *watching*, caught up in the sweep of a story that had the dimensions of a national epic.

Did someone other than Simpson murder Nicole? Was she really having an affair with the handsome young man who was murdered beside her? Was she faithful to her husband, or was she sleeping around? Was Simpson himself violent enough to murder two people? Was he physically strong enough to do it?

How was it possible that Simpson, such a modern, articulate, accomplished, elegant man (in many respects a lot like Othello himself), could murder his wife, Nicole, in a fit of jealous rage? It didn't seem to fit. In the trial of O.J., modern people were reencountering something they had repressed about themselves, perhaps something they wished did not exist. It was the reality that if provoked by jealousy and doubt, we still have the capacity to act in violent ways.

There were other characters in the drama. The judge, the lawyers, the witnesses, and the other characters in this national drama became celebrities to millions of people in North America and farther afield. They appeared in newspaper cartoons, became parodied on *Saturday Night Live*. Some, like Johnnie Cochran, parlayed their roles into prodigious income streams and celebrity.

Even after the verdict came in, people were still obsessed with this lurid tale of jealousy, obsession, delusion, passion, death, and shifting realities. Many people are still seeking answers today.

Through O.J., we see that jealous violence is part of our communal subconscious. Even when we do not experience the direct harm that jealousy causes, or when we are not violently jealous ourselves, it can erupt, as we will discover in the next chapter.

Murder and violence represent only a small part of the story. We also need to consider countless problems that obsessive jealousy causes in the lives of "normal" people who never lash out, never stalk or attack. These are the lives destabilized and crippled by obsessive jealousy, that never make the statistical summaries about crimes or divorces. Yet these ills are pernicious. And they are very real.

CHAPTER 2

THE DECEPTIVE POWER OF THE OTHELLO
RESPONSE TO DISRUPT OUR LIVES

When I first got jealous, I was taken completely off guard by what I was experiencing. It was like I was swimming in a calm sea when a tidal wave washed over me and swept me under and then carried me away. I experienced violent drives and emotions. I was someone I could barely recognize.

—A man named Dave discusses his first
encounter with the Othello response

PEOPLE WHO HAVE NEVER experienced obsessive jealousy have a hard time believing statements like Dave's. They find it hard to believe that jealousy can be that hard to control, that damaging.

Yet many people know otherwise. They are those who have locked horns with the Othello response, or spent time involved with people who suffer from it. Perhaps they have become jealous, or have fallen in love with someone who is.

People who have experienced the Othello response know that the power of jealousy is nothing to be trifled with. They know it can quickly become a force that is all but impossible to control.

WHEN THE OTHELLO RESPONSE STRIKES . . .

Could it be that obsessional jealousy is always slumbering beneath our loving relationships? Is it a shadow component of love, waiting to wake?

In different times and in different ways, most of us have experienced the power of the Othello response to send rays of keen doubt into our beliefs about ourselves and our love partners.

If you have ever fallen victim to jealousy, you will find that its emergence followed a plot line like this:

- *An unsettling event* caused you to doubt the fidelity of a current love partner or, sometimes, the fidelity of an *intended* love partner. The event could have been something like this:

- You saw your partner with some other person and did not know why they were together.

- You noticed changing patterns in a partner, such as increased or decreased interest in sex, changes in clothing or habits, or sudden interest in new pursuits.

- You found some documentation of possible infidelity, such as a charge-card bill and charges of phone calls noted on the monthly bill.

- You were suddenly reminded of a partner's previous love relationship, or perhaps some earlier partner suddenly reappeared on the scene.

- Some of us are more susceptible to feelings of jealousy than others at this stage. Certain people, in fact, appear predisposed to find cause to be jealous of their partners for very scant reasons—or, in extreme cases, for no reason at all. Other people have a higher jealousy "threshold." Unthreatened by and large, they are happy to have their partners spend time with other people who might possibly compete for affection. There are reasons why different people tend to sense sexual "threats" in different ways in their relationships.

- *You started obsessively fantasizing and worrying* about your partner's fidelity or infidelity. Your thoughts might have included:

- Fantasies of discovering your partner engaged in lovemaking with another person.

- Fears of appearing ridiculous or "cuckolded" in the eyes of people around you who know what you didn't: that your partner was betraying you.

- "Unmasking" fantasies in which you imagined revealing your partner's infidelities to other people, such as friends, parents, or children.

- Retaliatory daydreams of ways in which you could have gotten back at your partner by having an affair yourself, returning to a former spouse or lover, or simply having casual sex with someone outside your relationship. You might have acted out on these imaginings.

- If you are a male parent, worries that your children were fathered by another man.

- Starting to believe that by making yourself more attractive in dress, hairstyle, etc., you could influence your partner to stop "fooling around" and reengage fully in your relationship.

- Repugnance or hatred of your partner, made more Othello-like and intense by the underlying feelings of love you still possessed.

- Violent fantasies in which you envisioned the harm you would do to your partner, to his or her covert lover, or to yourself or to bystanders witnessing the problem, such as your partner's family, your children, etc.

- *Physiological changes and responses that replicate those that might occur if the imagined events had really occurred.* These might include physiological "flooding," which is manifested by increases in heartbeat, blood pressure, and adrenaline. Often, Othello reponse–related fantasies are so intense that they rival the intensity of responses to real problems, such as physical attack.

- *A loss of critical judgment.* The person who is suffering from recurrent obsessional fantasies becomes increasingly convinced that they are true. As in the play *Othello*, a new truth is constructed using selective facts as "proof" that an infidelity has taken place, while other facts are ignored.

- *Violent or tragic outcomes.* Fortunately, the Othello response is not always carried out to this tragic final stage. Some people are able to move beyond the problem when they learn that their suspicions have no basis. Others discover that their suspicions were justified, yet they behave in more moderated, emotionally mature ways by either working out the problems or leaving the relationship and moving on. Still other people will spend their lives stuck in the Othello response: mired in suspicions, unable to break free of obsessing about real or possible infidelities.

Some of these people, hopefully only a few, will act violently and carry the Othello response through to tragic outcomes.

THE TIP OF A BIGGER PROBLEM

The jealousy-induced murder and violent mayhem that we discussed in the last chapter, horrific though they may be, are only one part of the Othello response tragedy. Even when violent outcomes don't accompany the Othello response, a variety of other problems surface in our loving relationships and in ourselves:

- Some of us live lives of quiet desperation, constantly tormented by images of our partners' real or imagined infidelities.

- Others of us live with partners who are so jealous that we live in constant fear of the next eruption, the next distrustful episode.

- Some of us divorce because of jealousy's presence in our relationships.

- Some of us live in fear of violence from partners from previous relationships or marriages.

- Some of us, often for reasons that have roots in childhood or in earlier love relationships, become chronically obsessed with the fear that our partners will stray.

Worst of all is the fact that the Othello response doesn't only happen to other people. More often than we expect, it can happen to us.

IAGO WEAVES HIS PLOT

How is Iago able to quickly reshape the new love between Othello and Desdemona into a grotesque new thing made up of suspicion, jealousy, hatred, and murder?

The answer to that question is important, because Iago's wiles closely mirror the stages of the Othello response.

Iago's first try at revenge, after the principals arrive on the island of Cyprus, seems little more than a clever attempt to win the promotion he was denied before the play began. It's actually a rather clumsy plot: Iago will try to discredit Cassio by getting him drunk and then having his ally, Roderigo, a dishonorable thug, lure Cassio into a sword fight.

At first, this plot appears to work. Cassio quickly becomes drunk and Roderigo easily lures him into a raucous fight that is then stopped by Othello, who angrily dismisses Cassio from military duty for drinking and fighting while he is on his watch. However, Othello stops short of giving Iago the reward he was angling for, Cassio's newly vacated post.

Iago is only momentarily stalled by this setback. A brilliant improviser, he immediately launches a far more ambitious intrigue against Othello, resolving to convince him that Cassio is Desdemona's lover.

Iago seizes upon whatever he can to further his new plan. First he wins Cassio's confidence, portraying himself as a trustworthy confidant who is able to provide needed advice on how Cassio can regain his military rank. He urges Cassio to speak with Desdemona in private, where he can ask her to influence Othello to reinstate him. The trusting Cassio takes Iago's advice. He asks Emilia, Iago's wife and Desdemona's attendant, if he can visit Desdemona in her chambers. Emilia agrees and lets Cassio in.

Then as Iago and Othello return from inspecting battlements, they see Cassio leaving Desdemona's rooms. Iago mutters, "Ha! I like not that." When Othello asks what Iago meant by those words, Iago backpedals. He replies, "Cassio, my lord? No sure, I cannot think it, that he would steal away so guilty-like seeing you coming."

This is the first moment when doubt is triggered in Othello's mind, and a perfect depiction of the emotions we feel when an unexpected doubt causes pangs of doubt in our own minds regarding our lovers' fidelity. Did we see what we saw? Our sense of reality alters.

Iago continues to use every advantage to convince Othello that Cassio is having sexual relations with Desdemona. With apparent innocence, he asks Othello what role Cassio played in the days when Othello was secretly courting Desdemona. When Othello explains that Cassio served as a go-between for them during their secret courtship, Iago convinces him that Cassio's real intention at the time was to gain sexual access to Desdemona. Iago reminds Othello that Cassio is young, handsome, a white Venetian citizen. At once, Othello becomes convinced that Desdemona has betrayed him.

As Iago advances his plot, he is able to use the flimsiest of all things, an embroidered handkerchief that was Othello's first love-gift to Desdemona, as evidence that Cassio and Desdemona are lovers. Iago has Emilia steal this handkerchief for him. He places it in Cassio's chambers and then tells Othello that he has seen the handkerchief in Cassio's possession.

Othello takes the bait at once and asks Desdemona to lend him the handkerchief. She answers that she cannot. He tells her that if the handkerchief were lost, it would be an irrevocable loss. Frightened, Desdemona lies to Othello and assures him that the handkerchief is safely in her possession. Cassio, who is ignorant of the handkerchief's significance, gives it to his own lover, Bianca, asking her to make him a copy of it because he finds it to be beautiful.

Iago has now gained enough power over Othello that he can begin to drive his plot home not only with innuendo, but with outright lies. He tells Othello that Cassio has admitted having a sexual affair with Desdemona and suggests that if Othello will hide, he will overhear a conversation that will prove the infidelity once and for all. Othello hides within listening range as Iago asks Cassio about his relationship with his lover, Bianca. As Cassio talks of their love, Othello believes that he is referring to Desdemona.

Othello emerges from hiding and calmly inquires, "How shall I murder him, Iago?" He also asks Iago for advice on the best way to murder Desdemona. He asks Iago for poison, but Iago has another suggestion: Othello should strangle Desdemona: "Strangle her in her bed, even the bed she hath contaminated."

The suggestion pleases Othello, who is ready to murder his wife that very night. Iago requests the privilege of killing Cassio himself (in reality, he will goad gullible Roderigo into attempting that murder instead) and says he will report back to Othello before midnight.

That evening, Roderigo attacks Cassio, whose thick coat protects him from injury. In fact, Cassio wounds Roderigo, causing Iago to step in and stab Cassio, who falls to the ground. Othello happens to bass by and is pleased to see what he believes to be Cassio's corpse.

At the castle, Othello enters Desdemona's chambers. He stands at the foot of her bed, overcome with feelings of love for her. He says that he will not scar her face, but will kill her "bloodlessly." He kisses her and she awakens, asking her husband to come to bed. He orders her to say one final prayer and prepare for death. She begs him to tell her what she has done and he answers that she gave his handkerchief to Cassio, her lover.

When she asks him to summon Cassio, who can vouch for her innocence, Othello says Cassio is already dead. Desdemona begs Othello to let her live until the following day, but he refuses and smothers her. Emilia then bangs on the door, shouting that Cassio has been attacked, but that he is still alive. Othello conceals Desdemona behind her bed's curtains and lets Emilia enter. Desdemona, not quite dead, professes her innocence one last time. Emilia demands to know who has hurt her, and even in her final moment, Desdemona strives to protect Othello by saying, "Nobody. I myself. Farewell," before she dies.

Othello at first denies that he has murdered her, but Emilia does not believe him. He then admits that he is guilty, but only of sending a "liar gone to burn in hell!" Othello threatens Emilia to keep silent, but her courageous cries of "murder" awake everyone in the house. When Othello mentions the handkerchief, Emilia tells Othello that Iago made her steal it. Othello now glimpses the truth and lunges at Iago, but is promptly disarmed.

In another attempt to save himself, Iago grabs Emilia and stabs her. As she dies, Emilia says that Desdemona was chaste and in love with only the "cruel Moor." Iago runs away, but is quickly caught and returned as a prisoner. Othello pulls out a hidden sword and stabs Iago, inflicting only a wound before he is again disarmed. Cassio, though wounded, has now arrived in the room as well, and Othello asks him for forgiveness.

Othello pulls out a hidden dagger, stabs himself, and falls next to Desdemona. In his final moments, he kisses her and dies with the words, "I kiss'd thee ere I kill'd thee. No way but this. Killing myself, to die upon a kiss."

How long does it take Iago to accomplish his devastating deception? Critics and Shakespeare scholars differ in their view. Some believe that the play's action takes place within a time frame of a week. Others believe that everything is accomplished in only a few days. Harold Bloom, the eminent Shakespearean scholar, believes that Othello and Desdemona have not even had time to consummate their marriage by the time Iago has convinced Othello to kill his new wife. This, too, mirrors the force and quick effect of the Othello response. It has the potential to invade and destroy our worlds with devastating swiftness.

THE SUDDEN ONSET

Few of us are truly immune. Obsessive jealousy can suddenly strike most, if not all, of us, even if we have never had difficulties with issues of obsessive jealousy in the past. Here are the stories of a few people who fell victim to the Othello response in their lives. As you will notice, they are up-to-date, thinking people. They might bear more than a passing resemblance to you.

Jeanne's Discovery

Jeanne lives in suburban Chicago with her husband, John, and their two children. Last year, she was home from work one Monday when the mail arrived. She opened all the bills and, on an impulse, decided to open John's American Express statement too. She immediately noticed several odd, uncharacteristic charges on it. On his business trip to a convention in New York the month before, John had paid for three dinners at unusually expensive restaurants, meals in the $300 range. He had also spent $270 for tickets to the new show, *The Producers*. He couldn't have taken a group of clients to the show for that sum, she realized, just himself and one other person. *The Producers* was the hottest show on Broadway! Why hadn't John told tell her about it? What was he trying to cover up?

"It's nothing," she assured herself. But then, despite her attempts to keep calm, Jeanne started to have obsessive thoughts. Her mind began to generate lurid fantasies about her husband and another woman. She envisioned John sitting in an expensive restaurant with this other woman, enjoying a romantic meal. She imagined them in bed together. Images of infidelity kept flooding her mind. Sometimes the "other" appeared as blond, sometimes brunette, but always beautiful, and always very young. Jeanne began to compare herself to this imaginary woman, which she realized was absurd. *How can I be comparing myself to someone who I have imagined?* Jeanne wanted to know.

She tried to calm down, but she couldn't. She wanted to remind herself that she had no basis for becoming jealous until she had some verifiable information about John's actual activities on the trip. There was probably some logical explanation! But her mind continued to spiral through lurid fantasies that led right up to divorce, private investigators, confrontations with the other woman, telling their children that they were divorcing, even throwing John out of the house or doing him physical harm.

Then Jeanne noticed her husband's still-unopened cell phone bill. Maybe if she opened it, she realized, she would find that other woman's phone number! She could then call her up and confront her.

Suddenly, Jeanne's world was rocked to its foundation by obsessive doubts and uncertainty. On a quiet day at home, she suddenly discovered the primal, devastating power of jealousy, that green-eyed monster Iago told us about.

Jeanne also encountered something troubling about herself, a reality she would have rather not known. She discovered that she, like most of us, is capable of sudden, irrational, and powerful jealousy. She learned that the Othello response, sleeping silently, can suddenly destabilize our most cherished loving relationships, destroy our happiness, pull our families apart, and lead to violent imaginings.

This is only one story of jealousy's sudden emergence. Let's look at some more.

The Story of "Jason," High School Soccer Star

One day in the summer of the year 2000, a newspaper in an affluent New Jersey suburb near New York reported the story of a young man—let's call him Jason—who was a high school soccer standout and one of the most popular boys in his high school. The paper reported that when Jason learned that the girl he had been dating had been seen in the company of one of his teammates, Jason confronted this other boy at a party, pulled him out onto the front lawn, and beat him to the point where he needed to be hospitalized for a broken nose, fractured ribs, and internal bleeding. People in the town were astonished that a "good" boy would do such an atrocious thing. But there is an explanation. Jason, like Othello, got caught in the whirlpool of obsessive jealousy and couldn't swim free. Jason was too young and inexperienced to deal maturely with the emotions he was experiencing. He simply gave in to them, with disastrous consequences for himself, for two other students, and for his entire community.

Mary and Paul: Jealousy on a College Campus

A college student named Mary was dating Paul, also a student at her small college in the Midwest. She went home one weekend to visit her family, telling Paul she wouldn't return until Sunday. For some reason, she changed her mind and returned to campus on Saturday night, hoping to surprise Paul when she showed up unexpectedly. When Mary arrived at her dorm, she met Paul coming down the stairs with Jennie, her roommate. They looked flustered and Mary had a sudden conviction that they had been up in her room making love. With no premeditation, Mary swung the soft-drink bottle that was in her hand, opening a cut over Jennie's eye that required five stitches to close. The college community was thrown into an uproar by this violent act. The parents of all three of the students were called in. Again, people expressed shock that a "good" young woman had behaved in such an appalling and violent way. Mary, like Jason, didn't premeditate or plan her violent outburst. It just "happened." In an instant, she was overcome.

A Hike That Went Awry

Tamiko appeared to understand when her boyfriend, Jerry, got up very early one Sunday morning to take a daylong hike with some of his friends. But minutes after he left the apartment, a dark thought crossed her mind. Was it possible that he was leaving her so he could go have sex with another woman? The idea at first struck her as unlikely, but it grew in intensity as the day wore on. When Jerry didn't get back by late afternoon and the day began to darken, she became more and more convinced of the truth of her fantasy. In her mind, Jerry really was in bed with another woman! When he finally returned at dinnertime, she was an emotional wreck. Shaking and in tears, she confronted him with his "infidelity." Jerry, astonished, could only defend himself by offering to let Tamiko speak with his hiking friends. But Tamiko rejected that idea, because she already knew Jerry was "guilty." Nothing he could do would convince her otherwise. In just one day, the irrational jealousy of the Othello response had done irreparable harm to their relationship.

A New Lover Who Attracted Too Much Interest

Patricia attended a dinner party in Manhattan with Sandra, her new love interest who also happened to be a beautiful woman and a nearly famous theater director. All of Patricia's closest friends were there. The goal for the evening was to introduce Sandra to her "circle." Patricia had been looking forward to it, yet the evening quickly turned sour when Sandra became the center of attention. Even though Patricia realized she was thinking irrationally, she got furious at her friends for all the attention they directed at Sandra. Patricia began to compare herself to her friends and started to worry that one of them would "steal" her new lover. One of them seemed younger than she, another one prettier, another more artistic, etc. Patricia was in turmoil. Another sudden victim of the Othello response.

The Visitor at the Table

Michael, a divorced middle-aged man, was enjoying his second date with Monica, an attractive divorced woman. Despite his self-admonitions to keep cool and see how this new relationship would unfold, Michael found that he had become increasingly infatuated with Monica in the weeks since their first date. So for their second date, he invited her to one of his favorite restaurants and had high hopes for the evening.

Then, as they were waiting for their meal to arrive, a well-dressed man appeared at their table. Monica appeared to know him from her past. She was clearly happy to see him, and he was openly interested when she mentioned her recent divorce. After this man told Monica he would call her, Michael felt awful. He began to engage in obsessive worries about Monica, which intensified when she offered no explanation about this other man or about the role he played in her past. Michael's brain was racing. Maybe he had been counting too much on the idea that a long-lasting relationship would evolve with Monica. Maybe she was not ready to commit to a relationship. Maybe she was dating a lot of men, even having sex with them. Maybe he should ask her about this other man. (A bad idea, he decided. He didn't want to appear overeager or jealous, even though he *was*.) Even in this new, unformed relationship, the Othello response was displaying its unique power to unsettle and trigger obsessive, irrational thoughts.

Clothes Spark a Partner's Jealousy

Jack noticed that Scott, his lover for more than a year, was suddenly spending a lot of money on new clothes. In fact, Scott had changed from something of a slob to a very snappy dresser. Jack became convinced that Scott was "playing the field" and, without being able to stop himself, he began to spy on Scott by following him and calling him unexpectedly at different times of the night and day. Jack's life descended into a maelstrom of worry and doubt. He was behaving in ways that even he could not understand. Finally, in turmoil, he ended the relationship without ever learning whether his suspicions were true. His own emotions had made the relationship too painful to continue.

OUR NATIONAL SPECTACLES OF JEALOUSY AND INFIDELITY

We enjoy reading about marriages that are falling apart and watching relationships dissolve on TV. We dawdle before the *Jerry Springer Show* and similar programs as they parade people whose love lives are contorted into agonies of crisis. We watch robed television judges in their courtrooms, often dispensing justice to people who demand satisfaction from their former lovers or spouses. When such programs bring elements of violence or destructive jealousy, we tend to be fascinated even more. Then we have the recent wave of so-called "reality" television programs that purport to show groups of sexually viable young people who live together, start affairs, become jealous, have confrontations, and finally leave.

When we are asked to summarize the presidency of Bill Clinton, the first thing most of us think about is his infidelity to his wife and his affair with a young intern. After that, we go on to consider his economic policies and accomplishments, foreign policy, and so on. As we complete this book several years after Clinton left the White House, virtually all the media coverage he receives is tied to his extramarital exploits. As a nation, we care much more about them than about anything else he did, or did not do, during his eight years as a national leader.

We don't need to look long or hard to discover the central place the Othello response still occupies in our lives. But when this discovery has been made, our work has only begun. We need to ask one more troubling question: *Why?*

PART TWO
THE LIFE CYCLE OF THE OTHELLO RESPONSE

In the days when we were studying biology in high school, many of us learned the life cycles of different organisms. Insects began as eggs, moved on to be larvae and pupae, and finally emerged as fully formed adults. Before frogs earned their frogdom, they started out as eggs, then became adolescent tadpoles.

If we went to college and studied psychology, we discovered that human beings undergo their own evolutionary cycles too. We are conceived and we pass through distinct developmental phases in the womb. Then we emerge into the light of day to subsequently change into infants, toddlers, adolescents, adults, and aging old people. Finally, we die. It's all inevitable, unless we die early or suffer from some ailment that stalls us somewhere along the way.

It could be argued that dividing our lives up in this way is artificial. After all, each of us is only one person, not five or six, even though we change as we go through life. With the exception of puberty, most new stages emerge gradually, with no definite border between them. Yet understanding our life stages gives us a way to make useful, though imprecise, predictions about what will happen along the way "from cradle to grave." As toddlers, we can expect to fall down a lot, but to resolutely persevere until we walk and run. In puberty, we will experience radical physical transformations and the emotional withdrawal from our parents that prepares us for their exit from the stage of our lives. Imprecise as life cycles may be, they provide a rough script for our lives. Similarly, we can understand some of life's more dramatic processes better by breaking them down into predictable stages.

The author Elizabeth Kübler-Ross, for example, created one of the better-known, and more useful, life cycles. It is the DABDA model (standing for Denial, Anger, Bargaining, Depression, and Acceptance) she created to help people better understand the predictable stages that follow the death of a loved one, the diagnosis of a terminal disease, or any important life loss. The Othello response, like grief and all the other cataclysmic forces that sweep across our lives, has its own life cycle too. It passes through five distinct stages, which we will discuss in the following chapters. These are:

- Stage One: The Stage Is Set

- Stage Two: Gestation and Alienation, or the Ticking Time Bomb

- Stage Three: Unraveling—the Dangerous Drama Unfolds

- Stage Four: Confrontation, Accusation, and Denial

- Stage Five: After the Fall

Understanding where your relationship stands in this cycle can be a major help in taking corrective actions in a timely way. After all, not all "infections" of the Othello response result in unfortunate or tragic outcomes. We might become jealous or deal with a jealous partner, but not all of us will get divorced, leave our partners, or suffer from violent outcomes.

The fact is, the Othello response need not be fatal—either to the relationship or to its partners. Some of us are able to preserve, honor, and maintain our relationships, even when the Othello response has arrived in our lives. Others of us cannot, and suffer dire consequences. The difference is often a matter of understanding where we stand in the continuum of the Othello response—its life cycle—and taking timely action to make things right.

CHAPTER 3

STAGE ONE: THE STAGE IS SET

Imagine getting off work early and returning home. As you enter the house, you hear sounds coming from the back room. You call your partner's name, but no one answers. As you approach the back room, sounds of heavy breathing and moaning become louder. You open the bedroom door. On the bed is a stranger, naked and in the act of sexual intercourse with your partner. What emotions would you experience? If you are a woman, you would be likely to experience sadness and feelings of abandonment. If you are a man, you would be likely to experience rage.

—David M. Buss, *The Evolution of Desire*

"Nothing will come of nothing," as Shakespeare told us in *King Lear*. This observation holds especially true in human behavior and psychology. There are certain psychological precedents that make it more likely that we will evolve, or act, in certain ways:

- Men who become abusive in one or more love relationships are likely to do the same in later relationships too.

- When children suffer abuse, there is an extremely high likelihood that they will become abusive parents themselves.

■ Children of parents with addictive personality traits are much more likely to become addicted themselves — be it to alcohol, cigarettes, drugs, or gambling.

Sometimes, the precedents that usher in the Othello response are obvious. When a man or woman has shown a pattern of having affairs outside a primary relationship or marriage, that history will increase the likelihood that some kind of jealousy-induced dysfunctionality will occur within new relationships too. In her 1987 book *Women and Love*, author Shere Hite quotes one woman who, at age sixty-one, reported that she had many affairs during the course of a marriage that somehow lasted more than thirty years: "I have had extramarital affairs, twelve of them. One for two months, one for three months, one for one year, three for eighteen years, and one for thirty-three years. Many were concurrent; only two were exclusive . . . my husband did not know."

Even though this woman's marriage somehow survived that barrage, the presence of so many affairs, or of even one for that matter, clearly inflates the likelihood that some kind of jealousy will intrude upon a relationship.

Yet "sleeping around" is only one kind of precedent that boosts the statistical likelihood that the Othello response will invade. Let's take a closer look at some of the other patterns that can offer a reliable advance

MEN AND "MORBID JEALOUSY"

Morbid jealousy is a state in which men, and sometimes women, become obsessively jealous, even when there is no basis for suspecting their partners of infidelity. One possible explanation? People are so eager to take on new lovers that they concoct accusations of infidelity that give them the excuse they need to end their relationships and start new ones.

warning that the Othello reponse is likely to intrude on our loving relationships.

A TENDENCY TOWARD EXCESSIVE JEALOUSY IN ONE OR BOTH PARTNERS

Some people appear to be just "naturally jealous." As we will later discover in chapter 14, there are indicators that a tendency toward such behavior has become "hardwired" into our brains through human evolution, in which the most reproductively aggressive individuals won the game of natural selection. Even if such hardwiring is not the case, there is little doubt that some men and women have a tendency to engage in obsessively jealous behaviors concerning their partners. Some of these may include:

- Becoming uncontrollably obsessed with the idea that a partner will be unfaithful—even when there is no real basis for suspicion.

- Experiencing violent or hostile feelings for all men or women who appear to be interested in the partner—or who simply *appear*.

- Trying to keep a spouse or partner "concealed" from other possible sexual partners. This can mean preventing a partner from working or attending social functions.

- Abusing the partner, children who have resulted from the relationship, and any individuals who are perceived to be sexual "threats."

One young man, now divorced, describes patterns of

obsessive jealousy that existed even before he married his first wife: "While we were in college, we had a really white hot romance, really passionate. But then we graduated, I took a job in New York, and she got a job as a teacher in our suburban town. She was usually home by late afternoon, and seemed agitated when I arrived home several hours after she did each night. When I had to work late, she was more than merely upset. It suddenly dawned on me that she thought I was having an affair with someone at work, a belief that was supported when she began to make lots of unnecessary calls, and even unexpected visits, to my office. One night when I was planning to stay in the city to attend a basketball game with some male college friends, all her worries exploded into accusations when I arrived home. Our marriage, which was a youthful one, quickly dissolved. I later found out that her own mother had exhibited similar behavior throughout the life of her own marriage, over the span of more than forty years."

Yet such full-blown occurrences of the Othello response from the earliest days of a relationship are relatively rare. More often, jealous tendencies outlined above (to react violently to even skimpy hints of infidelity, etc.) are seething beneath the surface of one partner's consciousness. If he or she has such tendencies, the sad fact is that they will almost inevitably erupt into the relationship when the proper stimulus occurs, or simply without provocation as the relationship ages and changes take place.

WHY WE ARE OTHELLO

Through the years, many scholars observed that the character of Othello stands midway between Desdemona's naive innocence and Iago's cunning evil. He resembles those cartoon characters depicted with an angel on one shoulder and a devil on the other:

- Desdemona, the angel, is showing Othello the path of good.

- Iago stands on the other shoulder, feeding Othello lies. Unlike Desdemona, he doesn't offer truth, but only innuendo, half-truths, and false evidence.

Both this angel and this devil are present on our shoulders too. Desdemona is trust and belief in our partners, adherence to what is best in our love relationships when they are fresh, trusting, and new. Iago is also present in each of us. If we heed his voice and come under his power, we become seduced into destroying all that is good in our lives. Doubt, turmoil, and violent fantasies actually become preferable to love. The outcome of that kind of thinking is always tragic.

Finally, when Othello has accepted so many lies that he has lost all judgment, Iago tells Othello to kill his wife, and how to do it. Othello does not need that instruction; he already knows how to proceed.

"Failing at Fidelity" in Previous Relationships

Men who beat women are likely to do so again. Yet more subtle trends and tendencies can also be carried over from one loving relationship to the next, with the potential to trigger what might be called "serial dysfunction." Some of these tendencies include:

- *The presence of obsessive jealousy in previous relationships.* When the Othello response has crippled one relationship, it is more likely that it will occur again, especially if you have demonstrated a tendency to be excessively jealous. If a man or woman's previous relationships were stung by jealousy and doubt, there is every reason to expect that similar problems will intrude in subsequent relationships—unless, again, something in the person or in the nature of the new relationship is dramatically different from what has come before.

- A *history of secondary affairs while in previous relationships.* If your lover or spouse sought affection or sexual variety outside a primary relationship in the past, he or she might be likely to engage in similar behaviors again, unless something is dramatically different, or better, in your new relationship together. If you, conversely, are the person who has sought involvements outside your relationships, you are the one who is likely to do so again. Remember that such repeat patterns are not a certainty by any means. They are simply more likely to emerge.

- A *tendency to be "cuckholded" or betrayed.* On the surface, this factor seems illogical and counterintuitive. After all, when a person is betrayed by a lover, something has been done *to* him or her. He or she is a victim. Yet there is little doubt that certain people, for a complex set of reasons, tend to be stung by similar acts of betrayal from relationship to relationship.

These are only a handful of the ways in which earlier relationships' problems can be transferred to the next. There are others too. Again, there is no certainty that your new relationships will be unsettled by the same problems as your old ones, not even any guarantees that the Othello response will recur if it has struck you before. But if you have experienced it in past relationships, or encountered the problems we point out above, it would be wise to monitor them. They can be a reliable indicator that your relationship may "prequalify" you for infection by the Othello response.

PREQUALIFYING CONDITIONS IN THE FAMILIES OF ORIGIN
What kind of environment did you grow up in? How about

your partner or spouse? It is wise to consider these questions, because certain problems and issues that were present *then* are likely to reemerge *now* in your current relationships.

Abusive or addictive patterns, as noted, can be passed down from parents to children. We also know that the suicide of a parent is a strong predictor of suicide in his or her children. And patterns of relationship instability can be passed down too.

In short, events and behaviors we come to see as "possible" while we are growing up often unconsciously become our possibilities too. There's a subtle tendency to reenact old familial patterns. These can include:

- *"Straying" from the relationship.* When Dad or Mom slept around, for example, men and women develop a psychological "category" for that kind of behavior. They become more likely to engage in similar behaviors in their own adult years. Such behavior becomes acceptable and "normal" within that family system and tends to recur.

- *The presence of Othello response–like patterns in parents' marriages.* If your father or mother, or your partner's parents, suffered from obsessive jealousy or other aspects of the Othello response, it becomes more likely that the Othello response will emerge in some form in your adult relationships. Again, a "category" has been established for what your parents did or believed. You may discover an inchoate tendency in yourself to distrust your partner, or to subject him or her to excessive surveillance, or denigrate your partner so he or she will feel too unattractive to seek the affection of another suitor.

■ *Simple marital unhappiness.* When a child grows up seeing that his parents' relationship is unsettled and unsatisfactory, there may be an unconscious tendency to reenact that kind of marriage in adult life. And while unhappiness cannot be viewed as the Othello response per se, it can serve as a fertile breeding ground for many of the events that invite the Othello response into a relationship, such as flirting, fantasizing about other partners, or actual infidelities.

■ *Divorce.* The divorce of parents is always a difficult event for children. Even when it brings the dissolution of an unhappy marriage, it inevitably proves destabilizing to the children of the divorcing couple. When divorce is present in your family history or that of your partner, you have a category of divorce as a possibility and may believe that dissolution is more acceptable than do people whose parents remained married—even unhappily so. You may also be carrying the belief that a new relationship will bring you happiness.

CULTURAL OR SOCIOECONOMIC DIFFERENCES IN THE FAMILIES OF ORIGIN

Hollywood movie studios like romantic plots in which love unites two partners who come from very different cultural, national, or social backgrounds. The highly popular film *My Big Fat Greek Wedding*, for example, makes comic hay from the cultural clash that occurs when a young, working-class Greek-American woman marries an Anglo-American man from an aristocratic family. *Trading Places, Pretty Woman,* and other films have put lower-class prostitutes in the arms of aristocratic men. The list could go on and on.

Such cultural collisions make for entertaining movies, but

we also know that when couples come from very different backgrounds, considerable problems can arise. Consider these examples we've seen:

- *Krista*, a well-educated educator from a middle-class background, fell in love with Carlos, a Cuban-American whose entrepreneurial family had become very wealthy since their arrival on the American mainland. When Krista wanted to keep teaching after their marriage, she ran afoul of Carlos's family expectations that she would not work after their marriage.

- *Singh*, a Canadian man of Indian heritage, married Irene, a born-and-bred Canadian woman whose family had lived in the New World for generations. Cross-cultural frictions began to arise even before the wedding took place. Irene learned that according to Indian custom, her husband's mother (the mother of the groom) was expected to take a dominant role in planning the wedding and overseeing the creation of their new household as newlyweds. When Irene proved ignorant of these expectations, Singh's family convened a "war council" and told him that he had chosen an unsuitable marriage partner. That didn't set up a happy climate for the wedding or the marriage that ensued.

Such conflicting expectations are often so deeply ingrained that without keen vigilance and good communication on the part of both partners in the mix, problems can emerge. When a husband or wife fails to act in ways that his or her spouse has been expecting since childhood, accusations of incompatibility are quick to emerge. When one partner is threatened by such frictions, there is a certain likelihood that he or she will see the problems not just as incompatibility, but possibly as signals of infidelity too. As Singh tells us, "My family actually told me that Irene would soon take an Anglo lover after we got married, because she could not adhere to our beliefs and customs. For them, her inability to conform meant she was morally compromised. If I lacked the education and perspective to understand where those statements came from, I might have started to believe them myself and even suspected infidelity when Irene and I have encountered difficult periods together."

A Genetic Predisposition to Take Multiple Lovers

We have been unable to find any data to support the notion that promiscuous behavior on the part of a parent, if it remains unknown to that parent's children, will increase the odds of promiscuity in those offspring. In the lives of the authors, in fact, there is strong evidence to suggest that our two genetic fathers, and one of our mothers, were sexually active outside of the confines of their own marriages. And neither author, thankfully, shares those predispositions.

Yet Dr. Ken Ruge, a psychotherapist and coauthor of this book, has seen enough instances of this incipient trend in his counseling to believe that it merits consideration as a possible predictor of adult infidelities, especially in adult males. Sometimes, when a man is simply asked whether it is possible that his father might have done the same thing, that man begins to "put together the pieces" and recognizes a certain body of evidence that indicates that infidelities may have taken place.

Pending further research into this question, let us simply say that if it is possible that one of your parents engaged in extramarital affairs, that might be a tendency that will emerge again in your own adult life and relationships.

UNREALISTICALLY ROMANTIC BELIEFS ABOUT THE POWER OF LOVE

In many movies and books, romantic love is often portrayed as a cure-all for many of life's ills. Once the heroine and the hero have uttered the enchanted words, "I love you," their frictions seem to vanish in a rose-colored haze.

We need only look at some popular song lyrics to see how pervasive this magical view of love is:

- "Love will keep us together . . ."

- "Being in love with love . . ."

- "All at once am I several stories high . . ."

We often seem to believe that some starry hormonal feeling of love will guarantee fidelity. Such elation may be appropriate in the early days of a relationship, but problems can occur when we expect love's glow to exempt us from doing the difficult work that is often required to maintain a loving relationship or marriage. Even when we are in love, we need to be attentive to each other's needs. Even when we are in love, we still need to deal with finances, domestic routines, and all the other activities that subject a relationship to strain.

Even worse, an overly sanguine faith in the power of love can blind us to the fact that we or our partners might want to seek sexual or romantic liaisons outside the boundaries of the relationship. All too often, the fact that a couple has exchanged marriage vows or promises of commitment is taken as an iron-clad guarantee that a partner's exclusive affections have been secured.

At the risk of sounding cynical, excessive trust in a partner can blind us to the realities that problems that require our attention have intruded into our love relationships. Similarly, an excessive and naive trust can negatively steer us away from the very work that we need to undertake in order to make our loving relationships more stable, more durable, and more serene.

We're reminded of Colin, a man who placed such blind faith in his wife Leah's unswerving fidelity that he began to behave as though he had no responsibility to act romantically toward her. It was as though, through romantic love, he had put on blinders to the reality that Leah was still an attractive, sexually viable woman who was highly likely to attract the interest of other males. When Leah finally made it known to Colin that other men found her attractive, and that their attention to her was both flattering and sometimes tempting, Colin was shocked, and he had remedial work to do. Fortunately, before any infidelities had taken place, they were able to discuss their relationship and reintroduce some romance where it was needed to keep their marriage on track.

CHILDREN, CAREER, AND OTHER DISTRACTIONS FROM THE LOVE RELATIONSHIP

Our children and our careers are more than mere distractions. Yet the fact remains that when children are part of the picture, we sometimes deceive ourselves with the belief that investing unwavering attention and care in them will immunize our love relationships from harm from the outside. Both wives and husbands (who are caring for children more than they did in the past) often seem to believe that the love they invest in their offspring has a "trickle up" effect on their marriages.

That can be a damaging assumption. In years past, women

have often been stung when, after caring for and raising their children, their husbands have engaged in affairs or asked for a separation or a divorce. ("How could he engage in an extra-marital relationship, when I am investing all this care in the kids?") A similar delusion can set in where work is concerned. ("I know I've spent nearly all my time in the office for the last ten years, but doesn't my spouse understand that was an expression of love and care for my family?")

Other pastimes and activities also take needed attention away from our marriages and primary relationships. We know one man whose marriage became unglued after he had spent night after night working on volunteer activities for his town and his church, and also a nonworking woman whose social life with female friends became so engrossing that her husband began a string of casual affairs with women who "paid more attention" to him.

Balance is the key. We need to engage in activities that fulfill and complete us as individuals. At the same time, becoming obsessed with activities that lie outside our primary relationships could form part of a context where the Othello response can invade.

In summary, the precursor for the Othello response usually lies in one of these contexts, or in others that are unique to you, your partner, and your relationship. Or the precursor may be found in a *combination* of them.

CHAPTER 4

STAGE TWO: GESTATION AND ALIENATION, OR THE TICKING TIME BOMB

Othello: Why, what art thou?

Desdemona: Your wife, my lord; your true and loyal wife.

Othello: Come, swear it, damn thyself lest, being like one of
heaven, the devils themselves should fear to seize thee:
therefore be double damn'd. Swear thou art honest.

Desdemona: Heaven doth truly know it.

Othello: Heaven truly knows that thou art false as hell.

Desdemona: To whom, my lord? with whom? how am I false?

Othello: O Desdemona! away! away! away!

—*Othello*, Act IV, Scene 2

IN THE PRECEDING CHAPTER, we learned that Stage One of the Othello response life cycle is really a state of potentiality. Conditions exist that make it more likely that the Othello response will be triggered. Yet will potential, worrisome as it is, always lead to a full-blown onset of the Othello response? No. Many couples spend years, even their entire relationships, in Stage One. Despite the Stage One prequalifying conditions that make the Othello response likely, it never occurs.

What is needed to move from the potential to the reality, triggering Stage Two? Alienation within the relationship.

The breeding ground that allows this shift to occur can take many forms:

- "All the affection is gone from our relationship," one man explains. "My wife is at home with the kids and I'm orbiting out there somewhere, like the planet Pluto. All the warmth is in the middle, but I'm way out there somewhere, in the cold."

- "After years of playing second fiddle to my wife's career, something finally seemed to break in me," another man tells us. "Suddenly I felt totally alone. When I began an affair with another woman, people told me I had 'reached out' and taken a new lover. But it didn't feel like that. I wasn't moving out of my relationship with my wife, because that relationship no longer existed in any substantive way."

- "I still liked and respected my lover," a lesbian woman relates, "but I wasn't so surprised when she told me she no longer felt completely fulfilled in our relationship. It was hard news to take, but I think we both sensed a need to move on. We had just kind of moved apart."

Often, the following symptoms give a clear sign that this stage has begun. The possibility of actual infidelity is suddenly more real, as is the potential for one's primary relationship to dissolve.

RELATIONAL GRIDLOCK

There are a growing number of important issues that you and your partner are not discussing or taking action to correct. The issue at hand might well be one of these:

- Sexual issues surrounding the frequency or satisfaction of

WHAT WE EXPECT MEN AND WOMEN TO DO

Our families of origin teach us the way we expect men and women to act. Here are some assumptions people have reached, based on their early family experiences. Idiosyncratic though some may be, they appear to be normal to the people who learned them while growing up:

- "Men are strong, quiet breadwinners who put food on the table. They are expected to provide money and income for the family, but need not share their professional frustrations with their partners or children."

- "Men are emotionally alienated from the women in their lives, enjoying their real communication and friendship with men. Sports are the context where men bond closely with male friends."

- "Women are expected to become the caregivers for their own parents, and for their mate's parents, when those family elders grow old and infirm. Men just go to work."

- "It is odd and suspicious for married women to have friends who are men."

- "Women handle the rearing of children, but men discipline children when something goes wrong. Then women mediate and soften the hard positions their husbands take."

The things we observed during our formative years, and the things we were told, become a template for us in adult life. We often fall into similar patterns of behavior in our relationships.

sexual relations. "We haven't made love in more than six months, but I guess that is normal now that we are in our fifties," one man explains.

- Money issues, such as financial planning for retirement, spending, debt management, etc. Running away from problems often breeds new and unexpected problems in the areas of fidelity.

- Parenting concerns, frictions, and disagreements. It is not uncommon for one parent to "escape" marital problems by directing exclusive attention at the kids, who offer a sanctioned escape from a troubled or unsatisfying relationship.

- Issues concerning significant individuals on the periphery of your relationship, such as in-laws, aging parents, former spouses, or children from previous marriages or relationships.

- The diminishment of admiration and respect for the marriage. The memories and qualities of the relationship or marriage are beginning to change and become negative in the minds of both partners. Sometimes at this stage, partners mentally rewrite the history of their early years (often of their wedding and early marital years if they are a married couple), framing them as negative or ambivalent. "I had questions about my wife from the very beginning," a man says. "I recall, even walking down the aisle, having my doubts."

It is a troubling sign when subjects become taboo or off-limits in relationships. Sometimes such issues, though untouched, slumber on for long periods of time without doing much apparent harm to a relationship. However, the longer a serious issue is allowed to stew, the more it threatens to destabilize your relationship when it finally erupts through the surface.

OTHELLO THE OUTSIDER

The story of Othello is loosely based on a short tale about a Moor that appeared in a book of Italian stories that was popular in Shakespeare's time. Shakespeare changed many of the details in that sketchy story as he fleshed it out, even inventing Othello's name.

Yet why did Shakespeare choose to retain Othello's Moorish identity? Why not make him a Florentine (like Cassio, another character in the play), a Scotsman, an ancient Greek, or someone else familiar in his other plays? We believe that Shakespeare sensed some organic, psychological authenticity in the tale of a foreigner tricked into killing his wife by a citizen of his a new, unfamiliar country—something that he, Shakespeare, could amplify to the level of universal truth.

Of course, there is the obvious crowd appeal of having the central character be as exotic as one of a delegation of Moors that had been in residence at the English court only a few years before *Othello* premiered. But that was not all. By making Othello an alien in Italian society, Shakespeare intentionally made him stand apart from the world where he found himself. Like the Jewish Shylock in *The Merchant of Venice,* Othello is an outsider whose position grants us a vantage point from which we can discover unique insights about the world where we reside.

As an outsider, Othello is also inherently alienated from the world where he finds himself. The customs and societal expectations are alien to him. Like people who are in the throes of the Othello response, he is especially vulnerable to both personal insecurity and to the interpretations of reality that others provide.

The further that alienated people sink into their separateness, the more they can enter into a delusional world that is a false reflection of reality. In Othello's case, he allows the wrong person, Iago, to be the person who creates this new reality for him. Othello often calls Iago "honest," seeing him as a reliable arbiter of social actions and truths. He also calls Iago his "ancient," a needed repository of wisdom and knowledge that the Moor feels he lacks in his new terrain.

Othello is an emblem of the outsider in each of us. When things become uncertain or unsettled, we stand at the periphery of our world, looking in. When a partner's fidelity is the issue, we have the choice of loving and believing or hating and doubting. We can create our own inner reality from those events by imbuing them with our own beliefs, doubts, and suspicions.

This is treacherous new terrain. Like Othello, we can discover reality only after we have allowed tragic events to take place. Or unlike Othello, we can seek truth, recognize what is real, and save ourselves and the others around us.

AN INCREASE IN PSYCHOLOGICAL INFIDELITY

Research shows that many people, if not most, fantasize about becoming involved with people outside their primary relationships. But in Stage Two, a subtle shift takes place. The fantasizing is no longer abstract. In fact, it starts to resemble planning. Suddenly, you and/or your partner are no longer looking idly at attractive, alternative sexual partners. You are beginning to think about taking action on your fantasies. When your spouse is away next month, you really might invite that attractive divorced neighbor over for a drink and possibly more. Or on your next business trip, you really might try to have sex with an attractive colleague who will be traveling with your group.

This marks a significant shift. You are no longer just fantasizing, but really thinking about taking action on your attractions.

AN INCREASE IN SEXUAL OR ROMANTIC FANTASIZING ABOUT INDIVIDUALS WHO ARE NOT YOUR PRIMARY PARTNER

Perhaps you are often casting extrarelational individuals as partners in masturbatory fantasies. Or you might engage in an act of covert infidelity that appears to be common among both men and women: when making love with your partner, you imagine that you are having sex with someone else.

These covert infidelities are quite common. But if they become the norm or a daily pattern, you may be starting to plan to abandon your primary relationship. Or at the very least, you are acting as though that is what you are about to do.

So we see that as long as the essential loving bond between partners remains strong and active (as defined by deep familiarity, respect, and intimacy), the predetermining factors of Stage One are more likely to remain at bay. But when the essential bond between partners begins to fray in Stage Two, disruptive forces can gain momentum and finally win the upper hand.

EMOTIONAL INFIDELITY

For less impulsive personalities, another variation or symptom of this stage is emotional infidelity. One partner begins to have more of an emotional investment in a friendship outside the relationship than in the relationship itself.

In a marriage, this often occurs with a friend of the opposite sex. This friendship may lack an overt sexual component, but over time due to the increased loneliness in the marriage, this "special" friendship becomes extraordinarily important and an emotional focal point for the lonely spouse. The marital partner invests thought, caring, and feeling into this friendship that could be going into his or her marriage. Everything looks "normal" on the outside to the world, but the emotional affair is going on.

CHAPTER 5

STAGE THREE: UNRAVELING—
THE DANGEROUS DRAMA UNFOLDS

Wretched and foolish Jealousy,

How cam'st thou thus to enter me?

I ne'er was of thy kind . . .

Think'st thou that love is help'd by fear?

Go, get thee quickly forth . . .

I ne'er will owe my health to a disease.

—from "Against Jealousy," a poem by Shakespeare's
noted contemporary Ben Jonson

STAGE THREE BEGINS WHEN, through alienation and doubt, the foundation of your primary relationship becomes destabilized. Events may mark this transition, but at base it is driven by a profound psychological change. You could always count on the basic soundness of your relationship in the past. But suddenly, some fundamental shift has occurred. Things no longer "make sense" within the context of what has come before. There may be anger, but above all there is a sense of growing distance. You or your partner may be saying or thinking, "We're getting into a vacuum here. We're becoming estranged."

The words of the Beatles' song "I'm Looking Through You" give a fairly accurate depiction of what people feel

48

when they enter into this stage. Often, it is signaled in one of these two ways:

- *Growing apart.* A man named Doug explains, "Suddenly, after living with Manny for five years, I realized I didn't seem to know him anymore. I didn't know why we were still together. Even more troubling, I couldn't recall exactly what had brought us together in the first place."

- *A crisis erupts that brings the estrangement into the open.* Leila tells us, "I had always felt overrun by my husband's very successful, prosperous family. When my husband's wife and sister made the decision that we needed to move out of our house, which I loved, and into something more ostentatious and luxurious, I was furious. When my husband took sides with them, not me, I knew our marriage was doomed. Our values were at odds, but even worse, I suddenly saw that he was basically a stranger to me."

The transition to Stage Three is marked by different events in different relationships. Its arrival can be felt variously, in events such as these:

- A sudden sense that something is very different in your relationship. Perhaps you felt withdrawn from your partner in the past, but now you realize that you have grown completely apart. You may have felt suspicions about infidelity in the past, but now you suddenly "know" they are reality-based. As one woman at this stage in her relationship said, "We are living in a Bergman movie."

- New and uncharacteristic feelings offer proof of some fundamental change. Perhaps you realize that your partner, whom you always thought of as kind and caring, is now aggressive, critical, and unkind. Or that you no longer have any sense of his or her values, or that his or her friends do not seem trustworthy to you. In one way or another, your partner has become a stranger to you in ways that might not be repaired.

- Actual proof of infidelity lands at your feet. Perhaps you realize that you really don't know where your partner was last night, and the explanation is patently absurd. Or you open your partner's Visa bill and see that he or she has been living a "shadow life" you never knew about.

- Disagreements arise where they were never felt before. Perhaps your partner was always involved in parenting and domestic duties, and now loses interest. Or perhaps you feel tempted to withdraw. Again, something fundamental is changing in your relationship.

- A communication shift takes place. Perhaps you always communicated openly in the past and now your partner withdraws completely—or you want to do so yourself. Or perhaps you cut off your partner, or vice versa.

- Your partner has become defensive and sullen. He or she seems to feel tormented and is overly sensitive to criticism or minor observations.

Such changes do not come from nowhere. Let's take a

closer look at some of the events that happen to let the Stage Three "tiger" out of the closet and into center stage in our relationships.

EROSION

Sad to say, problems that we have the resilience to deal with in the short term sometimes wear our resolve away to the point where we give in and allow them to wash over us. "I put up with my wife's workaholism for more than five years," says Pat, a divorced man. "But the time finally came when I'd simply had enough. The kids and I hardly ever saw her, what with her working late nights and on weekends. First, after years of being patient, I lost my ability to stay that way. Then I lost my ability to be civil. I ended up behaving very badly, dating another woman and really tearing our marriage apart, while engaging in lots of self-justifications about why I was 'entitled' to act that way."

This man's words offer

CASE STUDY: "I NEED MORE TIME"

Jack met Nadia, a wonderful woman, when they were both in graduate school. He was pleased and gratified when they felt so close to each other that they began to have sexual intercourse regularly only a week after starting to spend a lot of time together.

But a darker side of the relationship soon emerged when Nadia expected Jack to spend all his waking and sleeping hours with her. And Jack, though he was interested in sex, was becoming devitalized by Nadia's nightly expectations that they have sex until the early hours of the morning hours. One night, Jack asked if they could refrain from having sex because he was too tired—a declaration that caused them to be up even later than usual, "ironing things out." A few days later, when he told her that he planned to spend the evening in his own home so he could study, the relationship nearly came apart completely. And a few weeks later, it did.

poignant evidence of the fact that unless problems are dealt with in a timely way in relationships, their destabilizing potential only grows.

EVENTS IN OTHER AREAS OF THE RELATIONSHIP

Changes in many significant life areas can exert a "ricochet" effect, suddenly causing boundaries to erode and the primary relationship to become destabilized. Some of these include:

- One partner experiences a health crisis or is diagnosed with a chronic disease.

- Children move out of the house to attend college.

- One member of the relationship becomes unemployed.

Even such seemingly unrelated events as automobile accidents and moving from one house to another have proven to be the catalysts that have sparked change in core relationships. In one suburban relationship, a domestic accident proved the catalyst. After a woman slipped and fell down a flight of stairs, to give one example, her husband proved unwilling to offer her the support she needed during a lengthy recovery period. After she recovered, she contacted a lawyer and began proceedings to "get him out of her life."

THE TEMPTATION OF ALCOHOL AND SELF-MEDICATING

Another temptation at this stage of the Othello response is that of self-medication. Because there is such a degree of loneliness and frustration and even contempt in the primary relationship or in the marriage, many people turn to alcohol, prescription medications, or illegal drugs as a way of blunting their pain. What this self-medicating often does is lay the groundwork for impulsive behavior and poor life choices, including sexual encounters with relative strangers, old flames, or others.

Drinking and drugging can also lead to violence, including homicidal and suicidal behavior, partly because one is neurologically impaired when one is self-medicating. As they say in AA, "There is no problem alcohol can't make worse." This is certainly true when we are dealing with a struggling marriage or relationship and the Othello response.

A New Context That Offers New Sexual Possibilities

A new job, an uptick in business travel, a move to a new city, a membership in a new organization—such occurrences inevitably expose us to interesting new people and the sexual possibilities they bring. Their presence can do one of several things to trigger the Othello response:

- We actually begin an affair with someone new.

- Romantic or sexual infatuations suddenly remind us of the fact that romance, sex, or other experiences we like and need are lacking or missing in our primary love relationships.

- The presence of possible new partners causes us to behave in uncharacteristic new ways that can trigger Stage Two of the Othello response in our primary partners. Perhaps because you are suddenly acting differently (dressing better, suddenly taking interest in new hobbies or interests), your partner "senses something happening."

One businessman relates an experience that brings such potential events into focus. "I've been traveling on business for years," he says. "But then on one five-day trip to a trade show, I suddenly developed a strong infatuation for a woman from another company. I noticed her in her company's booth. We had drinks in the hotel bar. We laughed. She reminded me of my wife when we were both younger. She roared at my old jokes, she found me interesting. I rediscovered a sexual part of myself that I had forgotten about in our marriage. We did not have sex, but when I returned home, my wife's radar told her something had happened, and she was right. Things were pretty ballistic in the house until we got things out into the open and talked them through."

A MOVE INTO ACTUAL INFIDELITY

Infidelity is the place where the essential nature of the Othello response shifts. You or your partner are not merely *thinking* about acting out on your attraction to an individual, or individuals, outside your primary relationship. Now, one of you is actually *doing something*.

That "something" can be a number of things. All relationships have their own internal rules and expectations regarding fidelity. Sometimes these rules are spoken, at other times unstated. Depending on their scope, betrayal can be construed to have occurred if either you or your partner:

- Engages in sexual relations with someone who is outside the relationship.

- Begins to date outside the relationship.

- Experiences physical intimacy that falls short of sexual union with someone outside the relationship.

- Plans to marry, or move in with, someone new.

As noted, couples define betrayal in different ways and draw different lines. To further complicate the issue, men and women sometimes define the "line" that cannot be crossed differently.

To see how these lines of demarcation can vary, let's consider these brief case histories:

- A man comes home from a business trip and tells his wife that while he was away, he invited a woman to his hotel room. He and the woman kissed, became physically intimate, but stopped short of engaging in sexual intercourse. This man's wife, though very upset and irate, nonetheless saw the problem as reparable.

- When a man learned that his wife had gone out on a date with another man, he contacted his lawyer and began divorce proceedings against his spouse. That date was all that was needed to signal to him that his primary relationship had dissolved.

The one thing that unifies all such happenings is the fact that one of the partners really believes that he or she has been betrayed by the actions taken by his or her counterpart. In this phase, you or your partner are not just fantasizing about becoming involved with someone new. One of you is actually doing so.

CHAPTER 6

STAGES FOUR AND FIVE: CONFRONTATION, ACCUSATION, AND DENIAL; AFTER THE FALL

Jake: What're you lookin' at? You lookin' at him?

Vickie: No, I'm not. I'm looking at you.

Jake: Don't tell me "No." I saw you lookin' at him. Why, you like him?

Vickie: I'm not interested in him.

Jake: You're not interested in him?

Vickie: No, I'm not.

Jake: In other words, you're not interested in him but you'd be interested in somebody else, right?

Vickie: Jake, c'mon now. Don't start.

Jake (to his friend Joey): I'd just love to catch her. Oooooh, I'd just love to catch her once.

> —an exchange in the Copacabana between Jake La Motta (Robert De Niro) and his wife, Vickie (Cathy Moriarty), from the movie *Raging Bull*, screenplay by Paul Schrader and Mardik Martin

IN THIS CHAPTER, WE will discuss two stages of the Othello response life cycle.

Confrontation marks the transition into Stage Four. After

all the uncertainty, the relationship reformulates in new, and always, disturbing ways. We suddenly hear statements like:

- "Okay, what is going on here? Are you having an affair?"

- "We're no longer together in this relationship."

- " I'm suspicious of you, and I never have been before."

Often, the statement's tone or content violates previously established norms for the relationship:

- A woman who is usually unassertive says, "Okay, what is going on here? Is our marriage over now?"

- A man who has been trying hard to keep the relationship stable suddenly breaks with the past and announces, "We need to be apart for a while. I've taken an apartment and am moving out."

In still more extreme circumstances, a person who has been unfaithful suddenly lays all the cards on the table:

- "I've fallen in love with someone else. I'm leaving you."

THE ALLURE OF A VIOLENT PARTNER

Shakespeare could have made his Othello the practitioner of virtually any profession he liked. Yet Shakespeare chose to make him not only a soldier, but a mercenary—the most violent kind of man and the most at home with war and killing. In Act I, Scene 3 of *Othello,* we also learn that Othello had a very troubled past that included imprisonment and slavery.

Othello himself tells us that Desdemona first loved him when she heard about this rather brutal past. ("She loved me for the dangers I had pass'd, And I loved her that she did pity them.")

Those words offer a glimpse into the kind of love experienced by this particular man and woman. It was a dangerous relationship to be sure, forged between a violent man and a kind, trusting woman. All it took was Iago, standing behind, to bring this beautiful love to a tragic conclusion.

ACCUSATION AND BLAME

Seeking to avoid blame is normal at this stage, and to be expected. Both parties, including the person who was unfaithful (if actual infidelity has occurred), need to place the blame for the impending dissolution of the relationship on the other person, and to try to remove it from themselves.

Outright arguments are to be expected, even in relationships where they never erupted in the past. Blame gets hurled back and forth in exchanges that can resemble a medieval battle where catapults are used to lob heavy stones back and forth across the armaments. The intention is to do the maximum amount of damage possible to the other party. At times like these, we hear statements like these:

- "You gave up on this relationship years ago. It was I who tried to keep it working."

- "You've been a lousy wife (or husband). Why have I spent years trying to keep us together?"

When mere accusations fall short, threats come into play—threats to hire rapacious divorce attorneys who will wreak financial havoc on the other partner, threats to prevent the children from seeing the other spouse, and on it goes.

CREATING THE OTHELLO "SCRIPT"

At this critical period, most people make statements to themselves, and to others, to convey the message that they have been wronged in the relationship and that they are therefore justified in taking action to end the relationship and move on. Sometimes the partners simply need to create a script they can use to tell other people what went wrong in their relationships.

If you have friends whose relationships have dissolved, you have doubtless heard the statement "My needs are not being met" at this critical juncture. You have also heard other reasons people give to explain why they are justified in moving outside their relationships. Whether it is true or not, some people accuse their spouses of the very thing they are contemplating: having an affair. Others accuse their partners of being bad parents or of being economically unreliable. The list could go on and on.

At times, all the complaints are justified. After all, no partner is perfect! Yet it is true that, when we are preparing to leave a relationship, the flaws and faults we happily accepted in our partners earlier in our relationships now become the fodder for scripts we use to self-justify our way into new territory. The chronic criticisms and contempt emerge so powerfully because all the goodwill and trust is gone!

SEEKING TO AVOID BLAME

With all the accusations flying around at this stage, a counterpart activity is to try to avoid blame:

AFFAIRS AS PARTING RITUALS

Both men and women sometimes use affairs as a catalyst to end relationships. By starting an affair or implying to a mate that such an affair has begun, they gain the freedom to leave the relationship and find new sex partners.

■ "You're nuts! You're making this up!" says a man whose wife has discovered that he has been having an affair behind her back. He is seeking to avoid blame at all costs. Perhaps he is telling himself that he can end his affair, cover up all the tracks it left, and keep his primary relationship going.

■ "It's all in your head! You're paranoid!" says a woman whose husband rightfully suspects that she is thinking of leaving him for someone else. It is clear she is not telling the truth. Her husband's confrontation and accusation came too early, before she had time to plan her own end to the relationship!

Suddenly, all rules go out the window. Troubling new questions ride into the relationship and take center stage:

■ Who's crazy?

■ Who's bad?

■ Who has been hurt more?

■ Who is more justified to do what has been done?

■ Who is to blame?

■ Who is the innocent party?

Everyone seeks to paint themselves as innocent. It is amazing to what length spouses and partners will go to avoid guilt or admit their part in the relational drama. At this stage, even seeking couples therapy can be a strategy for separation and the avoidance of guilt. Often the philandering partner leaves the vulnerable partner in the hands of a caring therapist before leaving the marriage or relationship.

It is rare for relationships at this late stage of the Othello response to be salvaged. As we will see in subsequent chapters, it can sometimes be done. In some cases, intervention and dialogue can repair the extreme damage that has been done. But the earlier that happens, the greater the chance that the relationship can be saved.

Let us not forget another variation of the Othello response: the truly paranoid spouse or partner whose sense of reality is warped by past trauma. In this case, the other partner may be totally innocent and falsely or repeatedly accused, abused, and eventually driven out of the relationship. This variant of the Othello response is difficult to heal and resolve. It involves intense therapy, both on an individual and couple level, and the identification of past trauma of the paranoid spouse. It also involves the unmasking the underlying happiness or loneliness in the marriage that may be the source of the Othello response drama.

STAGE FIVE: AFTER THE FALL

Now we move into Stage Five. Some kind of negative reformulation in the relationship has inevitably taken place in the wake of Stage Four. And both partners—whether singly or together—are entering into new territory.

At times, very dire times, this reformulation is accomplished through violent confrontation. The only way one partner can reinvent his or her world is to let the dark "Iago" aspect of his or her world take over completely. It is at such times that beatings, attempted murder, actual murder, and other violent acts are

WILL THE REAL STALKER PLEASE STAND UP?

Number of American women who were stalked by husbands and ex-husbands in 1997: 380,000

Number of American men who were stalked by a wife or ex-wife: 52,000

Source: Statistics compiled by *Divorce Magazine*

most likely to occur, victimizing the other partner in the relationship, children, property, a partner's real or imagined extramarital partners, or even simple bystanders of the relationship.

OWNING THE BLAME

It is surprising how seldom one member of a relationship at this stage admits to culpability in what has transpired to wreak such havoc in a relationship. Most often, both partners have much more invested in trying to justify their actions in the past and thereby divert blame from themselves.

In a small but significant number of instances, however, individuals who are brave enough to admit their own actions and accept blame can serve as catalysts that instigate healing in the relationship:

- "Okay, I admit it, I've been having an affair with a colleague for the last two years," a woman tells her husband. "It was wrong, it was terrible of me. I have hurt you very much and I hope we can try to rebuild our marriage."

- "All your suspicions were justified," a man says. "I have had a string of affairs and I feel awful about it."

Owning the problem in this way can be the most effective way to repair the relationship, when such repair is possible.

REBUILDING SEPARATE LIVES

When a relationship cannot be rebuilt—when the damage has been too great, or the possible remedies too ineffective to do enough good—healing takes place in the individual lives of both partners after they have dissolved the relationship.

Each survivor of the Othello response rebuilds his or her life in different ways. When one partner is especially predisposed to obsessional jealousy, there is a high likelihood that the problem will follow him or her to subsequent marriages or relationships. But there are other possibilities too. Where genuine incompatibility was the underlying cause of dissolution in the relationship, perhaps one or both partners might have learned lessons that can be applied to establish more security in later relationships.

This is why psychotherapy can be of great help at this stage in identifying the patterns of marital choice and marital interaction that can prevent the person from reenacting or repeating the same pattern again and again. This is also an important reason to act slowly in making a new marital choice. Often, people who have been involved in the Othello response drama are impulsive people. And sometimes, impulsive choices are poor choices. One strategy for slowing down is to become involved in a divorce recovery group for a number of weeks, where you can examine the early roots of the Othello response. You can look at your own marital history, your own family's history, and slowly come to a clearer sense of self-definition.

Slowing down gives you more opportunities to make better choices in terms of people and communication. It can also help you to avoid projecting your pain and disappointment onto the world. For example, many betrayed spouses make a "gender generalization" after their marriage ends:

- "All men are assholes."

- "All men want is sex."

- "All women are nuts."

If you come to accept such generalizations, they are sure to skew and color all your conceptions of the future in terms of what kinds of judgments you make. Perhaps you will avoid any relationships from now on. This is another reason why it might be a good idea to seek counseling or a recovery group of some kind so you can clearly understand the problems of your troubled relationship and place them in their specific historical context regarding your own marriage or relationship. The problems you faced were not about all men or all women.

In the tragic trajectory of the Othello response, we see a certain momentum that can destroy our relationships as surely as it destroyed Othello and his fragile world.

Yet not all of us will lose our primary relationships because of the Othello response. Intervention at the right time, in the right way, can interrupt the tragic flow and put us back in control of our lives. The earlier action is taken, the better.

In the chapters that follow, we will learn the outlooks and skills that can prevent the Othello response from wreaking ultimate havoc in our lives. In learning to honor our relationships and our partners, we have the opportunity to bring new happiness and fulfillment, both to ourselves and to the people with whom we have chosen to share our lives.

PART THREE
THE SELF-ADMINISTERED OTHELLO RESPONSE TEST AND COMMENTARY

You might already be all too aware that the Othello response is causing harm in your relationship and your life. Perhaps you are involved with a person who is obsessively jealous or even violent. Or perhaps it is you who feel intense jealousy toward your partner. Or perhaps you are facing problems in your relationship, not clearly defined, and would like to know whether jealousy might be a contributing cause.

The self-administered test and its scoring section (chapters 7 and 8 in this section) are designed to help you answer these questions. They are the first step to take to bring the problem under control. Only when the problem is understood can you apply the remedies to prevent the damage it can cause.

CHAPTER 7
THE SELF-ADMINISTERED
OTHELLO RESPONSE TEST

How LIKELY ARE YOU to fall victim to the Othello response in your current relationship? If the Othello response is already at work, how severe is the damage it is likely to cause? The following self-administered test will help answer those questions.

Please set aside about an hour to take this quiz. If your partner is also taking it, encourage him or her to set aside that much time as well. The questions are not complex, but since they deal with issues of jealousy and fidelity, an unhurried pace can help you mentally "recharge" as you go along and arrive at more thoughtful answers.

NOTES ON TAKING THE QUIZ

The most productive approach to taking this test is for both partners in a relationship to answer the questions separately, then compare their answers and scores afterward. If that is not comfortable or possible for you, taking the quiz on your own will also provide valuable information to help you assess yourself, your partner, and the risk posed by the Othello response in your relationship.

NOTE: You may download a working copy of this quiz at www.othelloresponse.com.

RESPOND TO EACH STATEMENT WITH A NUMBER
ON THE SCALE OF 1–5
1 *disagree strongly* . . . . 5 *agree strongly*

For further clarification:

- 1 means that you disagree very strongly with the statement given
- 2 means that you disagree with the statement
- 3 means that you are neutral or undecided about the statement
- 4 means you agree with the statement
- 5 means you agree very strongly with the statement

Try to have fun with this test and move quickly along. There are no wrong or right answers. A scoring section and commentary on each question follow at the end of the quiz.

NOTE: The term *partner* is used throughout this quiz to denote the other person in your love relationship, whether that person is a spouse, a boyfriend, a girlfriend, a lover, etc.

1) I might be angry or sad, but not terribly surprised to learn that my partner is romantically involved with someone other than me.
    disagree strongly 1 . . . 2 . . . 3 . . . 4 . . . 5 *agree strongly*

2) If I were unable to command the love and sexual fidelity of my spouse or partner, my sense of self-worth would be destroyed.
    disagree strongly 1 . . . 2 . . . 3 . . . 4 . . . 5 *agree strongly*

3) I think that some kind of violent revenge would be justified if my partner cheated on me.
    disagree strongly 1 . . . 2 . . . 3 . . . 4 . . . 5 *agree strongly*

4) Infidelity is one act that can never be forgiven.
   disagree strongly 1 . . . 2 . . . 3 . . . 4 . . . 5 *agree strongly*

5) I still harbor grudges against former partners with whom I am no longer involved.
   disagree strongly 1 . . . 2 . . . 3 . . . 4 . . . 5 *agree strongly*

6) I enjoy sexual fantasies about people other than my partner.
   disagree strongly 1 . . . 2 . . . 3 . . . 4 . . . 5 *agree strongly*

7) I probably would cheat on my partner if I were completely certain it would not be discovered.
   disagree strongly 1 . . . 2 . . . 3 . . . 4 . . . 5 *agree strongly*

8) When someone bumps into me while I am standing in line or cuts me off when I am driving, I react angrily and aggressively.
   disagree strongly 1 . . . 2 . . . 3 . . . 4 . . . 5 *agree strongly*

9) If I were in a position of greater power and influence, I would probably not be part of my current relationship.
   disagree strongly 1 . . . 2 . . . 3 . . . 4 . . . 5 *agree strongly*

10) When I suspect that my partner finds someone else attractive or interesting, I respond by belittling that person or trying to put him or her down.
   disagree strongly 1 . . . 2 . . . 3 . . . 4 . . . 5 *agree strongly*

11) I feel lonely in my relationship.
   disagree strongly 1 . . . 2 . . . 3 . . . 4 . . . 5 *agree strongly*

12) I sometimes think I am more attractive, or smarter, or better than my partner in some way.
disagree strongly 1 . . . 2 . . . 3 . . . 4 . . . 5 *agree strongly*

13) I really need to win my partner's approval and love.
disagree strongly 1 . . . 2 . . . 3 . . . 4 . . . 5 *agree strongly*

14) I am surprised that my partner chose me.
disagree strongly 1 . . . 2 . . . 3 . . . 4 . . . 5 *agree strongly*

15) I need to apologize at least once a week because I have become angry or jealous or have exhibited intimidating behavior.
disagree strongly 1 . . . 2 . . . 3 . . . 4 . . . 5 *agree strongly*

16) It is very important to me to know that I am attractive to people outside my marriage or primary relationship.
disagree strongly 1 . . . 2 . . . 3 . . . 4 . . . 5 *agree strongly*

17) If my marriage or relationship ended, I would land on my feet and not take too long to establish a new romantic tie.
disagree strongly 1 . . . 2 . . . 3 . . . 4 . . . 5 *agree strongly*

18) I believe it is permissible to have sexual relations with someone outside of my relationship without telling my spouse or partner.
disagree strongly 1 . . . 2 . . . 3 . . . 4 . . . 5 *agree strongly*

19) I sometimes consciously intimidate my partner by using harsh language, threats, aggressive actions, or aggressive body language.
disagree strongly 1 . . . 2 . . . 3 . . . 4 . . . 5 *agree strongly*

20) My needs are not being met in my current relationship.
   disagree strongly 1 . . . 2 . . . 3 . . . 4 . . . 5 *agree strongly*

21) My parents had a happy marriage.
   disagree strongly 1 . . . 2 . . . 3 . . . 4 . . . 5 *agree strongly*

22) By and large, I have never become restless in previous relationships.
   disagree strongly 1 . . . 2 . . . 3 . . . 4 . . . 5 *agree strongly*

23) I have never been involved with someone who became unnecessarily jealous of me.
   disagree strongly 1 . . . 2 . . . 3 . . . 4 . . . 5 *agree strongly*

24) I have always been involved with stable, reliable partner(s).
   disagree strongly 1 . . . 2 . . . 3 . . . 4 . . . 5 *agree strongly*

25) I have always been kind and nonabusive to my partners in previous relationships.
   disagree strongly 1 . . . 2 . . . 3 . . . 4 . . . 5 *agree strongly*

26) I have never been abused physically or verbally in previous relationships.
   disagree strongly 1 . . . 2 . . . 3 . . . 4 . . . 5 *agree strongly*

27) In previous love relationship(s), my partner(s) has (have) always been faithful to me.
   disagree strongly 1 . . . 2 . . . 3 . . . 4 . . . 5 *agree strongly*

28) My childhood was free from abuse.
   disagree strongly 1 . . . 2 . . . 3 . . . 4 . . . 5 *agree strongly*

29) In previous love relationship(s), I never "cheated" or had an affair.
disagree strongly 1 . . . 2 . . . 3 . . . 4 . . . 5 *agree strongly*

30) I have every reason to believe that my parents were faithful to each other.
disagree strongly 1 . . . 2 . . . 3 . . . 4 . . . 5 *agree strongly*

31) When confronted with an obstacle or setback, I feel challenged, not angry.
disagree strongly 1 . . . 2 . . . 3 . . . 4 . . . 5 *agree strongly*

32) My relationship with my parents is (or was) happy and calm.
disagree strongly 1 . . . 2 . . . 3 . . . 4 . . . 5 *agree strongly*

33) I like myself.
disagree strongly 1 . . . 2 . . . 3 . . . 4 . . . 5 *agree strongly*

34) I am just as good a person as my partner.
disagree strongly 1 . . . 2 . . . 3 . . . 4 . . . 5 *agree strongly*

NOTE: Answer the following question only if you are a biological father.

35) I have never harbored a fantasy, belief, or fear that my children were fathered by someone other than me.
disagree strongly 1 . . . 2 . . . 3 . . . 4 . . . 5 *agree strongly*

36) In his or her previous relationship(s), my partner was unfaithful or had a partner who was.
disagree strongly 1 . . . 2 . . . 3 . . . 4 . . . 5 *agree strongly*

37) My partner angers easily.
   disagree strongly 1 . . . 2 . . . 3 . . . 4 . . . 5 *agree strongly*

38) My partner's parents were unfaithful to each other when he
   or she was a child.
   disagree strongly 1 . . . 2 . . . 3 . . . 4 . . . 5 *agree strongly*

39) To keep my relationship strong, I need to try to be "different
   from" or "better than" my partner's previous partners.
   disagree strongly 1 . . . 2 . . . 3 . . . 4 . . . 5 *agree strongly*

40) I believe my partner was in a previous relationship where
   he or she abused someone verbally or physically.
   disagree strongly 1 . . . 2 . . . 3 . . . 4 . . . 5 *agree strongly*

41) I do not know my partner really, really well.
   disagree strongly 1 . . . 2 . . . 3 . . . 4 . . . 5 *agree strongly*

42) My partner was a victim of verbal, psychological, or physical abuse in a previous relationship.
   disagree strongly 1 . . . 2 . . . 3 . . . 4 . . . 5 *agree strongly*

43) My partner is still very angry at one or both of his or her
   parents, or with other relatives, because of past conflicts.
   disagree strongly 1 . . . 2 . . . 3 . . . 4 . . . 5 *agree strongly*

44) I do not look forward to time alone with my partner.
   disagree strongly 1 . . . 2 . . . 3 . . . 4 . . . 5 *agree strongly*

45) My partner is not satisfied in our relationship.
   disagree strongly 1 . . . 2 . . . 3 . . . 4 . . . 5 *agree strongly*

46) If you asked me what my partner is doing on a typical day when we are not together, I could not tell you in detail.
disagree strongly 1 . . . 2 . . . 3 . . . 4 . . . 5 *agree strongly*

47) Similarly, my partner doesn't know very well just how I spend my days when we are apart.
disagree strongly 1 . . . 2 . . . 3 . . . 4 . . . 5 *agree strongly*

48) My partner finds it especially difficult to apologize after arguments or disagreements.
disagree strongly 1 . . . 2 . . . 3 . . . 4 . . . 5 *agree strongly*

49) My partner and I are not very involved together in parenting, running a family enterprise, maintaining our home, retirement activities, or some other vital, shared interest.
disagree strongly 1 . . . 2 . . . 3 . . . 4 . . . 5 *agree strongly*

50) I have more invested in our relationship than my partner does.
disagree strongly 1 . . . 2 . . . 3 . . . 4 . . . 5 *agree strongly*

51) I know my partner has made a long-term commitment to our relationship.
disagree strongly 1 . . . 2 . . . 3 . . . 4 . . . 5 *agree strongly*

52) My partner is consistently kind and caring toward me and other people.
disagree strongly 1 . . . 2 . . . 3 . . . 4 . . . 5 *agree strongly*

53) I have never been afraid of my partner.
disagree strongly 1 . . . 2 . . . 3 . . . 4 . . . 5 *agree strongly*

54) There are very few things about my life that are hard for my partner to accept or understand.
disagree strongly 1 . . . 2 . . . 3 . . . 4 . . . 5 *agree strongly*

55) If I were to end my relationship with my partner or spouse, I would not be afraid for my safety afterward.
disagree strongly 1 . . . 2 . . . 3 . . . 4 . . . 5 *agree strongly*

56) My partner and I have worked through most, if not all, of the misunderstandings that have occurred in our relationship.
disagree strongly 1 . . . 2 . . . 3 . . . 4 . . . 5 *agree strongly*

57) My partner respects me.
disagree strongly 1 . . . 2 . . . 3 . . . 4 . . . 5 *agree strongly*

58) My partner and I have pretty much the same ideas about what a marriage (or committed relationship) is supposed to be.
disagree strongly 1 . . . 2 . . . 3 . . . 4 . . . 5 *agree strongly*

59) My partner believes that I am finished with my prior relationships.
disagree strongly 1 . . . 2 . . . 3 . . . 4 . . . 5 *agree strongly*

60) I find it easy to speak openly with my partner about what is on my mind.
disagree strongly 1 . . . 2 . . . 3 . . . 4 . . . 5 *agree strongly*

61) My partner never manipulates me.
disagree strongly 1 . . . 2 . . . 3 . . . 4 . . . 5 *agree strongly*

62) My partner does not make significantly more money than

I do. Similarly, I do not earn a great deal more than my partner does.

disagree strongly 1 . . . 2 . . . 3 . . . 4 . . . 5 *agree strongly*

63) I feel intimately connected with my partner when we are making love.

disagree strongly 1 . . . 2 . . . 3 . . . 4 . . . 5 *agree strongly*

64) I would be extremely surprised to hear that my partner had said something disparaging or disrespectful about me to his or her friends.

disagree strongly 1 . . . 2 . . . 3 . . . 4 . . . 5 *agree strongly*

65) My partner and I usually have similar emotional reactions in response to situations and issues.

disagree strongly 1 . . . 2 . . . 3 . . . 4 . . . 5 *agree strongly*

CHAPTER 8
INTERPRETING YOUR SCORE

WE WOULD URGE YOU to take your time as you consider your answers to the test you took in chapter 7. Also, it is productive to return to this chapter several times in the weeks and months ahead to reinterpret your answers. You will find that such "repeat visits" will open new perspectives in your answers, as well as new ideas and paths of inquiry.

INTERPRETING YOUR SCORES

As you may have noticed, the subject matter within this quiz is divided into distinct subject areas.

Section I: Your Attitudes (20 questions). Questions 1–20 deal with your personal attitudes regarding jealousy and infidelity.

Section II: Your Background and Experience (15 questions). Questions 21–35 deal with your background: the "baggage" of beliefs and expectations you bring to your current love relationship from both your family of origin and from previous love relationships.

Section III: Your Partner's Background and Experience (15 questions). Questions 36–50 deal with your partner's background and the "baggage" of beliefs and expectations he or she brings to your relationship from both his or her family of origin and from previous love relationships.

Section IV: Your View of Your Partner's Attitudes (15 questions). Questions 51–65 deal with your perceptions of your partner's attitudes regarding possessiveness and jealousy. Your answers cannot be completely accurate because you are answering these questions in your partner's stead. Yet your responses will prove useful and revealing—and after all, you probably know more about your partner's attitudes than you suspect.

To interpret your test, you will first calculate an average per-question score in each of these four sections, using the following worksheet.

SECTION I: YOUR ATTITUDES
(QUESTIONS 1–20; 20 QUESTIONS IN ALL)
Step One: Calculate your score for this section using this scoring table:

For each "1" response, award yourself 10 points.
For each "2" response, award yourself 20 points.
For each "3" response, award yourself 30 points.
For each "4" response, award yourself 40 points.
For each "5" response, award yourself 50 points.

Add up the sum of all your responses to questions 1–20 and enter it here on line one:

1. _____

Example: If on questions 1–20 your responses were 3, 3, 2, 5, 4, 1, 1, 3, 4, 2, 5, 3, 3, 4, 1, 3, 4, 4, 5, 2, you would enter the number <u>620</u> (the sum of those numbers) on line one.

Step Two: To calculate your average per-question score for this section, divide the total you entered on line one by 20 (the total number of questions answered) and enter the result here on line two:

2. _____

Example: Following the example above, your result would be <u>30.1</u>.

SECTION II: YOUR BACKGROUND AND EXPERIENCE
(QUESTIONS 21–35; 15 QUESTIONS IN ALL)

Step One: Calculate your score for this section using this scoring table:

> For each "1" response, award yourself 50 points.
> For each "2" response, award yourself 40 points.
> For each "3" response, award yourself 30 points.
> For each "4" response, award yourself 20 points.
> For each "5" response, award yourself 10 points.

Important: Note that questions in this section are given the <u>opposite</u> weight than in Section I.

Add up the sum of all your responses to questions 21–35 and enter it here on line three:

3. _____

NOTE: If you did not answer question 35, enter the total of your responses for questions 21–34.

Step Two: To calculate your average per-question score for this section, divide the total you entered on line three by the total number of questions you answered in this section and enter it here on line four:

4. _____

NOTE: If you did not answer question 35, divide the total on line three by 14 rather than 15 to calculate your per-question average score.

SECTION III: YOUR PARTNER'S BACKGROUND AND EXPERIENCE (QUESTIONS 36–50; 15 QUESTIONS IN ALL)

Step One: Calculate your score for this section using this scoring table:

For each "1" response, award yourself 10 points.
For each "2" response, award yourself 20 points.
For each "3" response, award yourself 30 points.
For each "4" response, award yourself 40 points.
For each "5" response, award yourself 50 points.

Add up the sum of all your responses to questions 36–50 and enter it here on line five:

5. _____

Step Two: To calculate your average per-question score for this section, divide the total you entered on line five by the total number of questions you answered in this section. Enter the result here on line six:

6. _____

SECTION IV: YOUR VIEW OF YOUR PARTNER'S ATTITUDES
(QUESTIONS 51–65; 15 QUESTIONS IN ALL).

Step One: Calculate your score for this section using this scoring table:

For each "1" response, award yourself 50 points.
For each "2" response, award yourself 40 points.
For each "3" response, award yourself 30 points.
For each "4" response, award yourself 20 points.
For each "5" response, award yourself 10 points.

Add up the sum of all your responses to questions 51–65 and enter it here on line seven:

7. _____

Step Two: To calculate your average per-question score for this section, divide the total you entered on line seven by 15, the total number of questions you answered in this section. Enter the result here on line eight:

8. _____

COMPLETE YOUR SCORING GRAPH
Use a line to mark your average scores in the following graph:

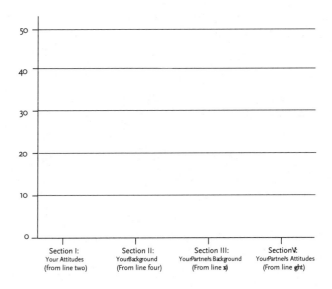

| | Section I:
Your Attitudes
(from line two) | Section II:
Your Background
(From line four) | Section III:
Your Partner's Background
(From line x) | Section V:
Your Partner's Attitudes
(From line ght) |

INTERPRETING YOUR SCORING GRAPH

It is normal, and expected, for most average per-section scores on the graph to hover in the 20–30 point average range, right in the middle of the scoring graph or slightly below. In fact, it would be highly unusual for the average score in any one section to exceed 40, which might point up an area of exceptional concern in your relationship. A average score of 42 in Section III, for example, would indicate that you are involved in a relationship with a person who you might not trust completely, or who brings a special degree of volatility to your relationship. Does that mean that you are involved with the "wrong" person, or that any relationship with your partner is unhealthy or inadvisable? Not necessarily; rather it means that you have discovered an area of susceptibility to the Othello response that requires extra thought, monitoring, and attention. Such high scores also point up areas where you and your partner should invest extra effort to communicate well, and respect each other's needs.

What about exceptionally low scores? They can be signs of a calm and secure area in your relationship. A average score of 18 in Section I, for example, means that you are in all likelihood a stable and reliable partner in your relationship. Yet low scores can still point up areas of potential susceptibility to the Othello response when they appear in marked contrast to higher scores in other areas of the scoring graph. For example:

■ A low score in Section I and a high score in Section IV means that you and your partner have quite different attitudes and behavior patterns that might trigger jealousy.

■ A high score in Section II and a low score in Section III might mean that you have more "baggage" on the jealousy issue than your partner does; it is you who might tend to become more jealous or obsessive on issues of fidelity than your partner.

Such contrasts, if they appear, are worth thinking about as you interpret the results of this quiz.

COMPARING RESULTS WITH YOUR PARTNER

If you completed this quiz at the same time as your partner, comparing your individual answers and your scoring graph can be an opportunity to increase the quality of your communication in your relationship and possibly open up some areas that, if discussed openly, can give cues to ways in which you can improve the quality of your relationship and communication.

If you are engaged in this joint exercise, be prepared for some surprises because we truly are not able to see ourselves as others see us! Some surprises might be in store for you both:

■ Perhaps your partner is afraid that you might be prone to obsessive jealousy or anger—and you were not even aware that he or she felt that way.

■ Perhaps your responses will let your partner know about dysfunctional patterns in your family that your partner did not know about. Again, this information could open up new areas for discussion, for helping each other, and for insulation against the Othello response.

There are many possibilities. The idea of sharing your score and results might at first seem threatening or embarrassing. Yet it is a step that, if taken, can initiate stimulating discussions and improve your closeness with your partner.

INTERPRETING YOUR RESPONSES TO INDIVIDUAL QUESTIONS

When taking this quiz, most people move ahead quickly, enjoy the process, and learn something. However, they also report two unusual reactions to the quiz:

■ They find that their responses to one or two questions are particularly troubling. Sometimes, the result leads to the discovery of an area of concern in their relationship.

■ They find a question puzzling or odd. What is the purpose of that question? they want to know. Why did we ask it?

For both these reasons, we feel it is important to offer some feedback and interpretation to the individual questions and what they might mean.

1) I might be angry or sad, but not terribly surprised to learn that my partner is romantically involved with someone other than me.

Most of us have no way of knowing exactly how we would feel if we discovered a partner's infidelity. The real point of this question is something different: to try to assess the level of trust in your relationship. Therefore, the key word is *surprised*. A numerical response of 4 or 5 indicates that you are having a difficult time trusting your partner. Trust is probably an issue you need to be working on.

2) If I were unable to command the love and sexual fidelity of my partner, my sense of self-worth would be destroyed.

This question assesses your ego structure. When issues of self-worth are tied too strongly to issues surrounding a partner's fidelity, that may be an indication that you are placing inappropriate pressure on your relationship by using it to gauge your self-worth. People who fall into such patterns are often more prone to the Othello response than people with a sturdier sense of self-value. Those of us who don't lean too heavily on our partners for ego fulfillment usually enjoy our relationships more and impose fewer unhealthy expectations upon our partners.

3) I think that some kind of violent revenge would be justified if my partner cheated on me.

This is a "time bomb" question, to be sure! Yet it is surprising how many people (men, especially, we need to acknowledge) feel that violence can be justified by a partner's unfaithfulness. A high score on this question indicates that, under some circumstances, you would think that acting violently would be permissible. We need to remember that Othello acted just this way. In fact, it was his intoxication with the possibility of violence that led him to overlook obvious truths about his wife's true nature. A high score on this question points up an area of personal vulnerability to making bad judgments and is an area of high concern.

4) Infidelity is one act that can never be forgiven.
We are not under any obligation to go through life forgiving all the wrongs that have been done to us! However, a high score on this question should serve as a cue to think closely about personal issues of assigning blame. This question also can embody a kind of inevitability; if you responded with a high score of 4 or 5, it is even possible you might be *expecting* infidelity on the part of your partner and already know how you will react. Approach this question, and your response, thoughtfully. You might have opened up a sensitive area that needs clarification and definition.

5) I still harbor grudges against former partners with whom I am no longer involved.
Grudges are a part of life. We don't need to forgive everyone. Yet a large number of grudges and "scores never settled" can be an indication that you actually expect things to go wrong in your *current relationship.* Could it be that you are waiting for your partner to do something blameworthy, so you can engage in the same pattern that disrupted previous relationships? Could it be that you want something to go wrong, so you can leave your current relationship and move on? We are not saying those possibilities are true, but this question points up some fertile areas for self-assessment.

6) I enjoy sexual fantasies about someone other than my partner.
Please don't beat yourself up about this one. As we were

writing this book, we discovered more than a few studies that indicate that many people generally do fantasize about sexual activities with people who are not their partners. It is something that men do more than women. However, this question is an invitation to consider the issues of sexual fulfillment and intimacy with your partner. A high score can indicate it is an area that needs to be communicated about and improved or the dissatisfaction that follows may lead to infidelities on someone's part in the future.

7) I probably would cheat on my partner if I were completely certain it would not be discovered.
This is a troubling question, to be sure. A high score indicates that you might need to consider some very fundamental issues about your fidelity beliefs. Are you being faithful only to avoid blame or endangering your stable relationship, or because you are truly invested in your partner? A high score might indicate some distance from your partner that could cause disruptions.

8) When someone bumps into me when I am standing in line or cuts me off when I am driving, I react angrily and aggressively.
This is a simple anger-assessment question. Although people who anger easily and quickly are not always prone to acting violently, they *are* usually quick to make the kind of bad judgments and decisions that might be precursors to the jealousy of the Othello response.

9) If I were in a position of greater power and influence, I would probably not be part of my current relationship.
This question, like #7 above, assesses your reasons for remaining

faithful to your partner. It also can point up the presence of some troubling self-assumptions and beliefs. If you believe your attractiveness and value reside in your power or material possessions, you are probably robbing yourself of the experience of a deeper relationship in which you and your partner connect on a deep and caring level. A high response of 4 or 5 indicates an area that needs consideration and rethinking in your life.

10) When I suspect that my partner finds someone else attractive or interesting, I respond by belittling that person or trying to put him or her down.
Again, this question points up personal insecurities that can make you susceptible to the Othello response. If your answer is high, that is an indication that you believe that your attractiveness hinges upon your ability to appear stronger or more successful than other people, rather than your own innate worth. It also indicates that you believe that it is what you *have* that appeals to your partner, not who you *are*. Again, this is an attitude that needs exploration and thought if you and your partner are to connect on a deep and intimate level.

11) I feel lonely in my relationship.
Loneliness when you are alone is one problem. Loneliness when you are supposed to be "with" another person can be an even more serious one. There are many reasons for loneliness within the context of loving relationships. It could be that your partner is a workaholic or engaged in a very demanding profession or career. (Or perhaps *you* are.) Whatever the reason, an answer of 4 or 5 indicates that you and your partner, though together or married, have failed to connect very deeply. Such estrangement is not only an indication of an

incomplete and unsatisfactory relationship; it can also be an invitation for misunderstandings, restlessness, jealousy, and the onset of the Othello response. If you feel lonely, or you suspect you partner does, it is time to make a fresh investment of time and energy in your relationship.

12) I sometimes think I am more attractive, or smarter, or better than my partner in some way.
The point of this question is not to determine whether you are a "bad" person who enjoys feeling better than your partner. Rather, it is here to help you uncover and assess two factors: 1) a feeling of alienation from your partner in a very important area, and 2) an area of incipient hostility or animosity. Both of these factors may be problems waiting to happen. If you dislike your partner, after all, you may latch on to flimsy evidence of infidelities in order to increase your anger and create a justification for leaving.

13) I really need to win my partner's approval and love.
Most of us strive to be worthy of a partner's affection and respect. However, a high response of 4 or 5 on this question may point up either: 1) incipient feelings of inadequateness on your part, or 2) that your partner is overly demanding or even manipulative of you. We know that many jealous individuals have been guilty of disparaging their partners' self-esteem in order to maintain sexual dominance over them. If that is happening in your relationship, it is a volatile state of affairs that may indicate jealousy on your partner's part.

14) I am surprised that my partner chose me.
This is an amplification of question #13 above. The most durable relationships are those in which both partners feel

largely co-equal, not in all areas of their lives, since all people are different (you might be stronger in parenting skills than your partner, for example, but he or she is stronger in some other area), but in most. If this is not the case and you feel generally inferior to your partner, that is an issue that needs to be addressed in your relationship. When a partner feels inferior or superior, that disparity often leads to dissatisfactions and temptations to stray.

15) I need to apologize at least once a week because I became angry or jealous or have exhibited intimidating behavior.

The willingness to apologize for wrongdoing is a good trait. However, if you are exhibiting behavior that requires frequent repentance on your part (either given or demanded by your partner) you are either: 1) a volatile person who has a tendency toward obsessive jealousy, or 2) engaged in a relationship with someone who takes offense unnecessarily and demands constant fence-mending on your part. Only you and your partner can determine which of these scenarios is at work, but it is a problem that needs to be corrected if your relationship is to remain balanced and strong.

16) It is very important to me that I am attractive to people outside my marriage or primary relationship.

Feeling capable and attractive is a good thing! However, a score of 4 or 5 may indicate that you place such a high premium on being attractive that you might be tempted to engage in infidelities if the right situation presented itself.

17) If my marriage or relationship ended, I would land on my feet and not take too long to establish a new romantic tie.

This is a complex question. While it is fine to feel confident that you could recover from any of life's major setbacks, a conviction that you would quickly enter into a new relationship may not be a positive sign. It may indicate an area of distance from your partner—even up to the level of feeling that "all men [or women] are essentially the same." If there is something special about your relationship, after all, it could not be so quickly replaced.

18) I believe it is permissible to have sexual relations with someone outside of my relationship, without telling my spouse or partner.
Like questions #7 and #9 above, this question assesses whether you are faithful to your partner because you want to be, or because of the trouble that would arise if you strayed. It points up an area that may need some consideration on your part.

19) I sometimes consciously intimidate my partner by using harsh language, threats, aggressive actions, or aggressive body language.
Intentional intimidation, whether good or bad, is a social tactic that some people use in their jobs or professions, or in certain social situations. Within a loving relationships, however, it has no place and indicates manipulative habits, not to mention a very real distance from your partner. A high response is a cause for consideration and possibly some discussion with a trusted friend or therapist.

20) My needs are not being met in my current relationship.
This is another time-bomb question. An answer of 4 or 5 indicates a high level of dissatisfaction on your part. The actions you should take depend very much on what those "needs" might be, in addition to how your partner is failing to meet

your demands in your relationship. Needs unmet, we know, are a strong indicator of friction and even eventual dissolution of relationships.

21) My parents had a happy marriage.
Research shows that the children of unhappy unions are more prone to create unhappiness in their own loving relationships when they reach their adult years. Parents' unhappiness is not a guarantee that you will be unhappy with your partner too— but a low score of 1 or 2 indicates that you would do well to be vigilant about your relationship, especially when friction occurs. Are you dealing effectively with the issues that need to be addressed in your own adult relationship, or bringing in some baggage from your past?

22) By and large, I have never become restless in previous relationships.
Sometimes, a history of restlessness in earlier relationships can be a simple sign that you were involved with the wrong people and that it was time to move on. A low answer of 1 or 2, however (especially if you are thinking of several prior relationships in which you grew restive), may indicate a behavior pattern you are likely to replicate when you feel it is time to move on and out of your relationship.

23) I have never been involved with someone who became unnecessarily jealous of me.
It is not necessarily your fault if previous partners were jealous of you! Yet the fact is, many of us tend to move from one relationship to another, replicating past problems and situations as we go. It might even be that you seek out partners who tend

to be jealous because you find jealousy flattering or positive. We are not saying that is the case with you, but it is a question worth considering as you assess your current relationship.

24) I have always been involved with stable, reliable partner(s).
This question is an amplification of #23 above. We often tend to bring the problems we encountered in one relationship on to the next and the next. You might be attracted to unreliable partners because they excite you, or stimulate your paternal or material attitudes, or fulfill some other need on your part. This question can help bring such patterns out into the open for consideration.

25) I have always been kind and nonabusive to my partners in previous relationships.
If you have exhibited abusive behavior before, you owe it to the health of your current relationship to be vigilant so that it does not occur in your current relationship. The intervention of a qualified therapist or counselor may be called for if you have a history of such volatile activity.

26) I have never been abused physically or verbally in previous relationships.
This is the counterpart to #25 above. Perhaps it is not your problem if you were involved with an abusive person in the past. But a high response of 4 or 5 should at least alert you to the necessity of protecting yourself by making sure you have not unintentionally become involved with someone who will replicate the abusive behavior you encountered in the past.

27) In previous love relationship(s), my partner(s) has (have) always been faithful to me.
As noted in responses to several questions above, we often

tend to encounter the problems in one relationship as we move onward into new ones. Hopefully the problems you came up against before will not return to plague you this time. But because people do tend to replicate old problems in new relationships, it is a possibility that may require vigilance on your part.

28) My childhood was free from abuse.

Many studies have shown that people who were victims of childhood abuse grow up to be abusive parents. Similarly, people who grew up abused often harbor anger and insecurities that can destabilize their love relationship when they reach their adult years. It can be a serious problem that demands the intervention of a qualified therapist.

29) In previous love relationship(s), I never "cheated" or had an affair.

If you did, that does not necessarily mean you are a "bad" person who cannot be trusted! Yet if you did engage in infidelity before, it is important to understand the underlying reasons. This knowledge may be essential to help you prevent similar problems in your current relationship.

30) I have every reason to believe that my parents were faithful to each other.

Parents' infidelities are certainly not a sure indicator that you too will stray from your love relationship and be unfaithful. Yet if infidelity was part of the "landscape" when you were growing up, you may tend to see such behavior as acceptable and permissible under certain circumstances. A low score of 1 or 2 on this question indicates, at the very least, that it is a potentiality on your part that may require vigilance.

31) When confronted with an obstacle or setback, I feel challenged, not angry.

Question #8 assesses a tendency to anger. However, in this question the key words in this question are "first response." If you tend to react to problems and suspected problems by first becoming angry, you may be cutting yourself off from the kind of calmer, considered thinking that can prevent inappropriate jealousy and the Othello response.

32) My relationship with my parents is (or was) happy and calm.

A high response of 1 or 2 may indicate an area of concern. People who are angry at their parents may be carrying "baggage" about certain problems that they will bring into their own love relationships as adults.

33) I like myself.

This question is a counterpart to question #13 above. Low self-esteem is a problem that can cripple relationships in many ways, including: 1) excessive dependence of a partner in order to maintain feelings of self-worth, and 2) a tendency to be overly suspicious of a partner's fidelity. These are problems to consider, discuss with your partner if possible, and possibly bring to the attention of a qualified therapist.

34) I am just as good a person as my partner.

This question is an augmentation of #33 above—an augmentation because you both feel like a person who is "not very good" but also someone who is "not as good" as your partner. A high response of 1 or 2 further underscores the commentary we offer there.

NOTE: Answer the following question only if you are a biological father.

35) I have never harbored a fantasy, belief, or fear that my children were fathered by someone other than me.

This is another time-bomb question! When men question their paternity, they often touch upon areas of great inner insecurity and anger too. The level of seriousness rises with the intensity of the way one questions one's paternity. If some years back you had a passing fantasy about what it might be like to learn that your children were not your "own," that is probably not a serious problem to address. If, however, you often doubt that you are the father of your children or engage in obsessive or violent fantasies about the issue, you might have encountered a problem that requires some real work to resolve if you are determined to strengthen and preserve your current love relationship.

36) In his or her previous relationship(s), my partner was unfaithful or had a partner who was.

We need to remember that we not only bring past problems to bear upon our current relationships. Our partners bring their own "baggage" too and can tend to re-create prior problems in the new relationships they create with us. Although those past problems might never recur, being aware of them can help us be more attuned to the issues of jealousy and the possible triggering of the Othello response.

37) My partner angers easily.

A high response of 4 or 5 might indicate an area of concern in your relationship. Anger can be a problem in its own right. An even more serious consequence of anger is the tendency to react angrily to life's obstacles instead of pausing to listen and reflect before acting. The result can be the kind of miscommunication that can usher in the Othello response.

38) My partner's parents were unfaithful to each other when he or she was a child.

See the comments regarding question #30 above. If your partner's parents "cheated" or roamed, there may be an increased likelihood of certain problems in your own relationship. Your partner too might tend to "roam," but that might be only one result of parental infidelity. Your partner, for example, might be looking for you to betray him or her, or might become exceptionally jealous and hurt at even small signs that you find someone else attractive.

39) To keep my relationship strong, I need to try to be "different from" or "better than" my partner's previous partners.

Most people hope things improve when they move from one relationship to another! Yet if you answered with a 4 or 5 because your partner often compares you to previous partners, you may be coming in for excessive pressure in your relationship. Depending on how intense this pressure is, you may simply become irritated, or angry, or even dissatisfied in your relationship. It is, again, an issue that needs to be aired and discussed with your partner if you are to keep your relationship strong.

40) I believe my partner was in a previous relationship where he or she abused someone verbally or physically.

A high answer of 4 or 5 indicates a strong area of concern, even though people do reform and self-correct. The problems of being involved with a person who has a history of being abusive are many. It could be that he or she will become abusive in your relationship too. It is also possible that, by being involved with such a volatile person, you are seeking to fulfill certain expectations or needs of your own, or replicating problems from older relationships in your current one. In any case, abuse is such a volatile issue that it needs to be considered and understood, not "swept under the carpet" until serious problems arise.

41) I do not know my partner really, really well.
A simple, but telling question. It is possible that you are in a new relationship and still learning. But over time, the "learning curve" should be such that you respond to this question with a low score of 1 or possibly 2. Intimacy and close knowledge of each other on all levels is the greatest insulator against incursions of the Othello response.

42) My partner was a victim of verbal, psychological, or physical abuse in a previous relationship.
This question is the "shadow side" of question #40 above; see our comments there. If your partner tends to replicate certain problems from one relationship to the next, there may be a likelihood that he or she will introduce the issue of abuse in some way into your relationship. Even if abuse does not become a problem per se, affiliated problems may arise. Your partner may project anger over previous relationships on you, for instance, or experience problems of low self-esteem. For this reason, a response of 4 or 5 on this question may point up an area that requires consideration and vigilance.

43) My partner is still very angry at one or both of his or her parents, or with other relatives, because of past conflicts.
See the commentary for question #32 above. People who feel unresolved anger in some of their most important relationships are more likely to introduce that anger into current relationships in destabilizing ways. Partners who are "cut off" from their families of origin may also be overly dependent on their partners for support.

44) I do not look forward to time alone with my partner.
Often, the most telling responses are elicited by the simplest questions and issues. If you do not look forward to being alone with your partner (if on Thursday, for example, you notice that you are dreading the coming weekend and the time you will have one-on-one), that is a clear indication that some troubling distance has occurred in your relationship. The reasons could be many. Some are normal, part of the "push and pull" of any relationship. It could be that you had one of your unusual arguments last weekend and that you have some making-up to do this time around. But if the reasons are chronic and ongoing (you argue, you are sexually incompatible, you just don't seem to *enjoy* being alone together), you may be living in a state of stasis that is an invitation to growing alienation and even the onset of the Othello response.

45) My partner is satisfied in our relationship.
A simple question, but a telling one. If you know or suspect that your partner is not satisfied in your relationship, you have encountered a troubling issue that requires airing, communication, and vigilance. The reasons we say that are many, and sometimes not too obvious. If you sense a partner's

dissatisfaction, it could be that your partner is not satisfied, and that may be an invitation to future problems. It may be that you only *believe* your partner is not satisfied and that you are projecting your insecurities upon your partner. Or perhaps you are not satisfied and are misunderstanding what your partner feels and believes. For such reasons, a high answer of 4 or 5 should serve as an invitation for some consideration and communication.

46) If you asked me what my partner is doing on a typical day when we are not together, I could not tell you in detail.
A high answer of 4 or 5 on this question may point up a common, and often overlooked, invitation to suspicion, misunderstanding, and many other problems associated with the Othello response. Closeness and a clear knowledge of a partner's activities are two of the greatest insulators against the kind of suspicions that can trigger or strengthen the Othello response.

47) Similarly, my partner doesn't know very well just how I spend my days when we are apart.
See the comments about question #46 above.

48) My partner finds it especially difficult to apologize after arguments or disagreements.
When couples are not able to "make up" and heal after arguments and rifts, that can be a strong indicator of problems to come in the relationship. When problems are never resolved, just allowed to fester, a relationship is far more likely to become destabilized.

49) My partner and I are not very involved together in

parenting, running a family enterprise, maintaining our home, retirement activities, or some other vital, shared interest.

A high answer of 4 or 5 on this question may be an indication of a situation in which you are somewhat alienated from your partner, which can be a prescription for many of the difficulties that can trigger or worsen the Othello response. When people are in a relationship but not intimately connected in important life activities, they can become detached ("together but not together") in ways that can open up possibilities for both infidelity and misunderstandings surrounding the issue.

50) I have more invested in our relationship than my partner does.

A high answer of 4 or 5 is a cause for real concern. If you feel you are "giving" more than your partner, it could be that it is the case. It could also be that you believe you have unfulfilled expectations for your relationship or that you and your partner are not communicating about needs and visions for being together, or other issues.

51) I know my partner has made a long-term commitment to our relationship.

Another real cause for concern. As noted in our comments for question #50 above, a score of 4 or 5 on this question may mean that you have uncovered a real problem: your partner is not as invested in your relationship as you are. But a high score can mean other things too, such as a generalized lack of satisfaction on your part or personal insecurity. Again, it is an issue that would benefit from discussion and thought.

52) My partner is consistently kind and caring toward me and other people.
A high score of 4 or 5 provides a real cause for concern. The level of severity depends on your experience in your relationship and on the level of your partner's rudeness. Some of us are able to sustain relationships with people who sometimes, but very seldom, become angry and rude.

53) I have never been afraid of my partner.
Because fear and love cannot easily exist side by side, a high score of 4 or 5 can be a real cause for concern. There are many reasons why people in love relationships can come to fear each other, ranging from fear of jealousy to fear of economic, sexual, or other aggression. A high score of 4 or 5 indicates that *your* needs are not being met in your relationship—needs for happiness, stability, intimacy, and security. To not only enjoy a better loving relationship but also to experience a more positive existence overall, it would be advisable to consider the basis of your fears, confront them openly, and take needed measures to bring things right.

54) There are very few things about my life that are hard for my partner to accept or understand.
No two people understand or accept everything about each other. Yet a high score of 4 or 5 on this question can be an indicator of unhealthy distance between you and your partner. It might be a good idea to bring to light the areas where you most acutely feel distant from your partner (possibly over issues of parenting, finances, religion) and discuss how their resolution might have a positive impact on your ability to feel close to your partner. We do know that incipient feelings of alienation have a way of worsening over time, sometimes

triggering feelings of jealousy and opening the way for the disturbances of the Othello response.

55) If I were to end my relationship with my partner or spouse, I would not be afraid for my safety afterward.

As we noted in the commentary for question #53 above, love and fear do not easily coexist in a relationship. There is an additional troubling aspect to this question too — the fact that some people remain unhappily in relationships simply because they fear the dire things that might occur if they took steps to move away or move on. For this reason, a high answer of 4 or 5 on this answer can be a real cause for concern and a strong indication that important issues of trust remain unresolved (and, hopefully, capable of being resolved) in your relationship.

56) My partner and I have worked through most, if not all, of the misunderstandings that have occurred in our relationship.

Lack of forgiveness, a strong predictor of relationship failures, festers and destabilizes relationships over time. For this reason, a high response of 4 or 5 points up a real area of concern. This problem is complex, however, and may require considerable care to resolve. If your partner has not been able to forgive you, it might be helpful to try to understand why. Is that lack of forgiveness a manipulation intended to control you emotionally, possibly gain control over you and your activities? Is it an indication that your partner has some very real insecurities and needs that require attention and discussion? The possibilities are many, but ought to be understood and addressed if your relationship is to remain stable and strong.

57) My partner respects me.

Respect is an important word in a relationship. When you are respected, that means your partner feels you are a worthy individual: worthy of esteem, worthy of his or her affection, worthy of being accorded the independence and liberty that an adult person deserves in a loving relationship. For this reason, a high score of 4 or 5 can be a real indicator of an area that needs opening up and examination.

58) My partner and I have pretty much the same ideas about what a marriage (or committed relationship) is supposed to be.

If this is not the case, it is important to clarify expectations and dreams. Do you know what you are signing up for in your relationship? Are you and your partner "on the same page," or pursuing different goals for your relationship. A low score of 1 or 2 may indicate an area that needs more communication and attention.

59) My partner believes that I am finished with my prior relationships.

On the surface, this question is a simple trust-assessor. If your partner thinks you are still attracted to former lovers or partners, that may be a very real issue you need to open up and resolve. On deeper levels, this question can uncover more complex issues, such as a partner's finding excuses to avoid establishing intimacy with you, or even expressing a desire to engage in infidelities him- or herself. To keep your relationship strong, it is important to get to the root of the feeling that your partner distrusts you; then, if possible, address and rectify the causes of that distrust.

60) I find it easy to speak openly with my partner about what is on my mind.
A simple question, but telling. On the surface you may wonder why we put it among those designed to assess your *partner*'s attitudes, not in the sections about yours. It's because when we feel unable to talk freely about our concerns with our partners, it is usually because we fear retribution or disapproval — in other words, something about our partner's attitude is causing us to self-censor.

61) My partner never manipulates me.
If you marked a score of 4 or 5 for this question, it could be that your partner is manipulative; or it could simply be that you feel that way. In either case, you have encountered an area of strong dissatisfaction, and possibly anger, in your relationship together. If you feel demeaned or manipulated in your relationship, you owe it to both your own happiness and to your relationship's health to understand and address the causes.

62) My partner does not make significantly more money than I do. Similarly, I do not earn a great deal more than my partner does.
When one partner earns a great deal more than the other, that scenario can create another potential "time bomb" of resentment on the part of the "breadwinner," who feels he or she has been taken advantage of, or deserves a greater "say" about things. After all, it is their money that is paying the bills. Unequal financial power can also breed resentment in the "low-wage" partner who may feel controlled, guilty, or put into a position of forced gratitude. If equivalent earning can't be achieved, it is essential to clearly communicate about areas of responsibility and create a strong sense of "we-ness."

63) I feel intimately connected with my partner when we are making love.

Because it is sometimes normal not to feel fully engaged in lovemaking, feelings of distance or estrangement during sex are not always signs of a harmed or dysfunctional relationship. However, if you often feel estranged from your partner during lovemaking (which is a time when you can justifiably expect to feel not only pleasure, but acceptance and comfort as well), that might be a sign that distance has intruded into your relationship in destabilizing ways. In relationships that are fundamentally sound, such problems usually resolve through unpressured, open discussion between partners. Above all, it is important not to wait until incipient sexual incompatibility becomes more acute.

64) I would be extremely surprised to hear that my partner had said something disparaging or disrespectful about me to his or her friends.

This is a simple barometer of the level of respect and confidentiality you feel in your relationship. The main point of this question is actually not whether your partner says unkind or disparaging things about you to his or her friends, but whether such an event would prove surprising to you. If it would not—if you scored this question with a 4 or 5—you might do well to step back and evaluate the level of respect you feel you deserve and receive in your relationship. A lack of faith in a partner's respect for the confidentiality of your relationship can be a problem that can worsen over time and lead to feelings of estrangement and anger.

65) My partner and I usually have similar emotional reactions in response to situations and issues.

As with question #60, you may wonder why we placed this

question here, in the section about your partner's attitudes and not in the sections about *your* attitudes. In reality, this final question of the quiz assesses feelings of distance on *both* sides of your relationship. If your partner is a stranger to you, then the opposite must also be true. A high score of 4 or 5 on this question may indicate incipient or growing alienation that can be an invitation to misunderstandings, suspicion, and the jealous machinations of the Othello response.

PART FOUR
PREVENTATIVE MEASURES AND CURES

Is the Othello response truly unstoppable? Is it like one of those movie monsters that "keeps on coming" no matter how hard or long we battle against it?

Usually not. Granted, there are times when one partner in a relationship has become so overcome by jealousy, or has such a tendency to become so, that there is little hope for the relationship. There are also times when some disruption takes place (one partner goes outside the relationship for love, for example) that does such harm that the relationship cannot be mended.

In most cases, however, the Othello response can be prevented or controlled:

■ While our relationships are sound and healthy, we can take steps to keep the Othello response at bay and inoculate ourselves from it.

■ When our relationships become unsettled by jealousy, we can often take steps to heal them and recover.

Let's take a closer look at how these goals can be reached to keep our loving relationships sound, stable, and safe.

CHAPTER 9

LEARNING TO MANAGE
VIOLENT JEALOUSY

Over the past six weeks, law enforcement officials say, four women have been killed by soldiers stationed at Fort Bragg, three of them members of the Special Forces who had been fighting in Afghanistan. Local police officials and military commanders at Fort Bragg say there was no relationship among any of the soldiers and no connection between the killings and the Special Forces or the men's assignments in Afghanistan. But Deborah D. Tucker, the co-chairwoman of the Defense Department's Task Force on Domestic Violence, said, "This does feel really unusual to have so many partners killed in such a short time in one place."

While some soldiers here say the stress of separation and fears of infidelity by wives may have contributed to the killings, Ms. Tucker said the real explanation was more likely a history of trouble in the marriages—including some previous violence— combined with husbands who craved control and felt anxious about losing it during deployment in Afghanistan.

— "Wife Killings at Fort Reflect Growing Problem in Military,"
by Fox Butterfield, *New York Times*, July 29, 2002

CAN ANGER BE POSITIVE? It can. In its positive manifestations, anger serves as a call to self-preservation and to the preservation of others, and to energetically address injustices and wrongs.

Here is a short list of notable examples of positive anger. We're sure you could add more:

- Sir Winston Churchill was enraged when Britain came under attack from Germany in World War II, but he used that anger to lead his country in a highly effective and inspirational way.

- Mother Teresa was angry at poverty, but she turned her anger into positive action to help the poor.

- Dr. Martin Luther King was angry about the oppression of African-Americans and adopted the strategies of passive resistance to achieve major change in America.

But we all know that most anger is destructive, not constructive. In many of our lives, anger is present, yet it provides no benefits at all. It is little more than a chronic destabilizing force, sometimes close to an addiction, that leads us to turn away from what is best in ourselves and what is most to be cherished in others.

It is not surprising that anger infects so many of us today. We live in an angry age. At work, we are often enraged at our employers, at our bosses, at our colleagues, at our customers, and at the people who work for us. In stores and banks, we are impatient and become irate at the people who cut ahead of us in line or who take too long in line. While going to and from work, we are indignant at other drivers, at the other passengers who share the train, at the train company itself. At home, we

ANGER-MANAGEMENT SUGGESTIONS FROM THE AMERICAN PSYCHOLOGICAL ASSOCIATION

■ *Relax.* Breathing deeply, meditating, and conjuring up relaxing mental images can help calm anger. So can stretching and yoga. The APA states that the most effective approach is to practice these techniques daily, not only when anger strikes.

■ *Try cognitive restructuring.* In other words, change the way you think. Angry people often engage in thoughts that are dramatic and exaggerated. If you have this tendency, try to replace those thoughts with more rational ones. *Example:* Instead of saying, "You never listen to me!" when you encountering a problem with your partner, say, "Can we please take a few minutes to talk about this?" The APA states that "logic defeats anger, because anger, even when it's justified, can quickly become irrational . . . Remind yourself that the world is "not out to get you," you're just experiencing some of the rough spots of daily life.

■ *Solve problems.* Anger is sometimes caused by inescapable problems in our lives. When facing one, make a plan and check your progress regularly. If you are trying to correct things head-on, you will feel better able to solve such problems and feel calmer.

■ *Communicate better.* When anger hits, slow down and try to think through your responses before you speak. When you are criticized, make an effort to listen instead of fighting back or becoming defensive.

■ *Use humor.* Trying to laugh at a problem can help defuse its hold over us. The APA recommends "silly" humor. If you are tempted to call a colleague a "dirtbag," for example, draw a picture of what a bag full of dirt looks like. The APA, however, cautions against trying to "laugh off" problems without dealing with them, and also against sarcastic, harsh humor, which is just another expression of anger.

■ *Alter your timing or environment.* If you and your spouse tend to argue at night, for example, try to discuss sensitive issues at another time of the day. Or if your daily drive to work leaves you enraged, take a different route or means of transporttion — or negotiate to arrive at work at a later hour.

are furious at the telemarketers who call and interrupt our dinners. We are cross at the bills that come in.

Such anger has become an expected part of life today. There is another kind of anger that has become commonplace today also, the anger that many people feel today toward their partners in love relationships. That anger can be either small or great. Like the reasons behind it, it can be either great or small. Yet the damage it does to us and our loved ones is rarely minor. Often, it can take on catastrophic dimensions.

SIMPLE LOVE IS NOT SO SIMPLE AFTER ALL

Scholars and readers have often disparaged Desdemona for her one-dimensionality. Critics with feminist orientations, in particular, have cast her as little more than a pawn in a play about men, written by a man.

Such views are not without foundation. Desdemona does nothing to save herself and little to defend herself. Finally, she lies down and allows herself to be killed and, with her last gasp, actually takes the blame for what has happened to her.

Yet is Desdemona just a pale pawn in a larger male game? She certainly walks a simple, unerring path. She loves Othello and she does not waver, even when she is publicly called a whore by her husband and shocked by events that quickly transform her fresh new marriage into a terrifying and alien world.

Even at the point of death after Othello's final attack, she refuses to implicate him and says instead that she attacked herself. It is a statement that on the surface works as a defense of her husband, but surely resonates on deeper levels.

Shakespeare, through her, may be telling us that we all cast our own fate. By loving without wavering, she participates in her own end. She could have fled or gone back to her father's house, or gone to the duke and asked for protection. But a simple, clearer path was her choice, despite its peril. Desdemona remains steady, and in that constancy lies her remarkable purity and strength as both character and psychological model.

No, the fact that Desdemona has singularity of purpose and purity of heart does not mean she is weak or insipid. Hers is the pure and shining path that lies open to us—the path that runs in the opposite direction from the one that Iago also opens before us.

Desdemona is all things good. She is the decision to remain steady and constant and committed to those we love. She is the decision not to give in to the voice of jealousy or doubt. She is the inner voice that, even when we are in the midst of jealousy and doubt in our love relationship, calls us back to our first days of purity and commitment and innocence and certitude. In her simplicity lies the greatest strength of all.

GENERAL ANGER AND SPECIFIC JEALOUSY

Anger, once it starts in one area of our relationships, can act like a flash fire that spreads quickly into other areas of a relationship. For reasons we'll explore in depth in later chapters, amorphous anger that has little to do with infidelity or jealousy per se can still trigger issues of jealousy and the Othello response:

- When one member of a relationship becomes sufficiently angry with the other partner, he or she may begin to suspect (or accuse) the other of infidelity, or of harboring sexual interest for other people. The reasons are complex. At times, the "accuser" needs to direct blame at the other person as a way to deflect it away from him- or herself. Something is going wrong with the relationship, and it must be the other person's fault. Such jealous feelings can function as a self-fulfilling prophesy: "If I am this angry at my partner, there must be a reason. And that reason is that my partner is no longer faithful to me."

- At other times, one partner may use anger as a justification for seeking sexual or romantic liaisons outside the primary relationship. At these critical junctures in relationships, we often hear the "wandering" partner use the old cliché: "I sought the company of someone new because I was not getting what I needed at home."

- Such affairs often serve as "exit strategies" to help one partner leave a relationship that has become unhappy or hostile. Instead of investing the time and energy to understand why he or she bas become so angry and make things better, one partner simply destroys the relationship and starts another one. Sometimes this "exit" pattern tends to be repeated from one relationship to the next.

Kim and Bob

Kim and Bob met while they were attending graduate school at Yale. Kim was in law school, Bob in drama school. Five years later, Kim was a successful attorney in New York. Bob was still trying to get his big break as a playwright. Kim was making a lot of money and Bob was making nearly nothing. Kim was able to live with the arrangement for a time, but her growing frustration over their economic situation soon changed to outright hostility toward Bob. Even when he had a play go into production and it seemed that he was about to move ahead in his career, she was still too angry at him to reinvest their marriage with acceptance and love. With no evidence to support the idea, she accused Bob of sleeping with one of the actresses who was appearing in his new play. In fact, she had already begun an affair of her own with another attorney who worked in her firm. One day Bob went to the bank and found that Kim had withdrawn all the money from their joint checking and savings accounts. When he asked her about it, she told him that she knew he had been having an affair, and acted on the advice of a divorce attorney. She demanded that he move out of their apartment. Kim's affair ended shortly after her divorce from Bob was finalized. It took some years before she was able to accept the idea that she had used accusations of infidelity to end her marriage and that anger over money was the real destabilizing force.

Jim and Lorraine

Jim didn't know why, but a few years after he married Lorraine, he began to get increasingly mad at her. The annoyance started small, then grew. When she became pregnant, he became unexpectedly very angry about her changed appearance and sexual unavailability. Then after the birth of their two children, he began to stew over all the time she needed to invest in mothering instead of being with him. He grew angrier and angrier. Then, five years into their marriage, Jim's father got cancer and died. For some reason, this was the event that pushed Jim's anger over the edge. Because a channel for his anger had already been established—Lorraine—he directed his fury over his father's death at her too. He grew suspicious and began to accuse her of infidelity: an absurd notion, since she spent almost all her time at home with the children. He then started to hit her. Lorraine sought help and the marriage quickly dissolved.

From Work Frustrations to Jealousy

Liz had a history of acting angrily and aggressively toward colleagues at work, drivers on the road, service people, and many other people too. For a time after she married a calm and kind man named Sam, she felt calmer in general, and didn't become angry at him. About two years into the marriage, however, things changed after Sam lost his job. Liz soon became openly angry with him. No matter how much he did to find a new job, it was never enough to allay her anger at him. Before long, her anger took on a very unkind aspect. She used what she knew about his own insecurities to attack him with especially devastating accuracy and cruelty. Sam, predictably, began to withdraw from the relationship, realizing that the more he shared with Liz, the more he made himself vulnerable to her attacks. Soon, Sam got back in touch with a comparatively kind and gentle woman he was dating before he met Liz. First he only felt the need for some compassionate company, but an affair soon began. Sam soon asked Liz for a divorce and their marriage dissolved.

"Blocking Off " to Prevent a Partner's Anger

Paul and Harold, two gay men, experienced a similar problem. In their case, they were both chronically angry individuals. Only a few months into their relationship, they had both begun to "block off" areas of their lives where they realized they were especially likely to trigger angry reactions from each other. Paul, in fact, was still grieving after the death of a previous lover, yet he realized he could not mention his remorse without throwing Harold into a jealous rage. As more and more areas of anger, and fear of anger, began to take over the relationship, it ended.

So we see that unconsidered anger often leads to jealousy and outbreaks of the Othello response. How can we find our way out of this highly potent, dangerous morass?

THE ROOTS OF JEALOUS ANGER

If chronic anger has already infected our loving relationships, can we keep it from destabilizing our relationships in even more damaging ways? Before we can consider the answer to that question, we need to pause and consider the nature of anger itself.

"THERE IS NO PROBLEM DRINKING CAN'T MAKE WORSE"

In the play *Othello*, Iago understands that the only way he can lure the honorable man Cassio into a brawl and discredit him is to first get him drunk. One again, Shakespeare is airing a fundamental human truth: Alcohol leads to impaired judgment; its abuse can lead to irrational jealousy and violent behavior.

This reality, in fact, gets reported on the evening news whenever we hear that perpetrators of violent crimes were "drinking heavily" before murder and mayhem began.

Even when alcohol abuse does not lead to violence, it can still damage our love relationships. As Alcoholics Anonymous says, "There is no problem drinking can't make worse." In the distorted world created by alcoholism, jealousy can easily take hold.

Alcoholism is a daunting and destabilizing foe whose life disruptions often include these:

- Mood changes, including increased anger, irritability, and violent outbursts.

- Personality changes, including jealousy and paranoia.

- Evasiveness, including a need to hide evidence of drinking.

- Missing work and experiencing problems on the job.

- Loss of interest in activities that were previously enjoyable.

- Loss of interest in food.

- Injuring oneself or others while intoxicated.

- Carelessness about hygiene and appearance.

- Lack of concentration, confusion, and memory loss.

- Money problems caused by drinking.

If you are often angry, or if your partner is, it is important to consider where your anger patterns and your drinking intersect—and to seek help when appropriate. Remember, help may be needed.

Evolutionary psychologists tell us that there are clear reasons why anger, like jealousy, has evolved among humans. Anger had an important role to play in the self-preservation that led our ancestors to survive and, by extension, to preserve their genetic line:

- Angry, more aggressive ancestors were better able to compete for food and other needed resources.

- Similarly, they were better able to compete for mates and, once paired, intimidate and keep away sexual competitors.

- Primal anger, like fear, provided a powerful physical stimulus that enabled our forbears to fight off physical threats from enemies and natural predators.

In the social structures of primates and other animals, anger and aggression function much like the "coin of the realm," a medium for the holding and transfer of power. This fact is illustrated clearly in many studies of primate social structures, notably the book *Chimpanzee Politics* and the other writings of the noted anthropologist Frans de Waal. Dr. De Waal has spent years observing the social structures among lower primates. He has found that, among chimps at least, the most aggressive and battle-successful males rise to the alpha position in their communities and remain there enjoying free sexual access to females until a younger male either intimidates the older male or fights him to win the alpha position. This unseating is sometimes brought about through political intrigue. Toward the end of his regime, a weakening older alpha male will sometimes retain power for a time by exchanging favors with a few stronger, younger males. For example, he will allow them sexual access to some of the females; in exchange, they will help him intimidate potential candidates trying to rise to the alpha position. Soon, however, such alliances crumble as the alpha male eventually proves to lack sufficient aggressive power to retain his position. Often, the allies he cultivated turn on him and claim positions of power for themselves.

These are not pretty scenarios. They reveal attitudes and behaviors that ideally should not exist in humans. After all, we are called "higher" primates. Yet the fact that such hostile patterns may be lurking in our genetic background does not prevent us from making the decision to behave in better ways. When we are chronically or senselessly angry with our mates, we might be harboring emotions that are "natural," in the sense that we have a genetic predisposition for them. But that does not mean that we are powerless to resist them. After all, when we are in a marriage or love relationship, it is rare that we need to expend so much energy and aggressive force to "stay in power" or fend off our partners' real or suspected suitors.

ANOTHER WAY ANGER KILLS

In 2002, the journal *Circulation* reported the results of a study conducted by psychologist Janice E. Williams at the University of North Carolina at Chapel Hill. Dr. Williams and her colleagues were exploring whether people with chronically angry dispositions were more prone to heart disease than were nonangry people. The study was extensive, gathering data on heart disease among 12,986 white and African-American men and women aged forty-five to sixty-four.

A questionnaire assessed which subjects had a tendency toward frequent, long-lasting, and intense rages. Four and a half years later, Williams and her colleagues checked to see which participants had experienced heart attacks or other cardiovascular problems. The results were striking. People with high scores on the anger scale were three times more likely to have suffered heart attacks or sudden cardiac death than were those with low scores.

Anger, in fact, was found to have more of an effect on mortality than smoking, being overweight, or having diabetes.

Then, too, there is the fact that anger, like jealousy itself, feeds upon itself and is highly seductive. When we allow it to gain a hold over us and our relationships, we are giving in to an inefficient, unevolved way to go through life. We are acting like Othello and make ourselves vulnerable to the possibility that we too might destroy what is best in our lives.

Curbing Chronic Anger

If you are a victim of chronic anger, you are dealing with a very specific personality problem that is, in all likelihood, doing damage to your ability to fully engage in a loving relationship. It may be harming your spouse, partner, or your children. Even if you are bottling up your anger and holding it in, it is acting as a severe stress, doing considerable damage to you and probably to those around you, in ways that may be hard for you to discern. At the very least, it is robbing the pleasure from what should be one of the most uplifting and joyous experiences in life: sharing your life with another person.

Studies conducted in the 1980s at Duke University Medical Center, and follow-up studies since, have determined that 20 percent of all adults suffer from Chronic Anger syndrome. For reasons that are still under investigation, sufferers are prone to experience anger as a first reaction to many of life's routine events or obstacles:

- When chronically angry individuals encounter other people who are less intelligent, ill, or otherwise disadvantaged, their first tendency is to become angry with them, not compassionate.

- When chronically angry people find themselves behind

slow drivers on the road, they have little ability to reach back, take a deep breath, relax, or find reasons to empathize with the person who is driving slowly. Instead, they feel victimized and believe they are justified to react in an uncivil, hostile way.

■ When chronically angry people hear that someone has been the victim of a crime, their first reaction is hostility toward the perpetrator. Compassion for the victims might follow, but usually as an afterthought.

How can you tell if you are chronically angry? The Minnesota Multiphasic Personality Inventory (MMPI), a psychological test developed more than sixty years ago, can help determine your habitual level of anger and hostility. In fact, the Hostility Scale of the MMPI has become such an accepted tool, courts sometimes require that it be administered to divorcing fathers who are embroiled in custody disputes. If the test uncovers elevated levels of habitual anger and hostility, fathers may be denied custody of their children and even visitation rights.

If you wonder whether excessive anger and hostility may have gained a hold over your life, another tool for self-investigation is to engage in a simple self-evaluation. One effective approach is simply to keep a personal log of your own anger for one week. During that time, carry a small "anger notebook" with you and jot a note every time you become angry at someone or something or simply have a negative, angry thought. At the end of each day, review your notes and look for patterns:

■ Are there certain activities that cause you to become unnecessarily angry?

■ Are there certain times of day when you are most prone to feel angry? Where are you at those times?

■ Is your anger tied to the use of alcohol or other substances?

■ Is the level of your anger appropriate to the problems that trigger it, or is it not?

■ If you become angry at your partner or spouse, what specific actions on his or her part are likely to trigger that reaction?

■ Does jealousy or the fear of your partner's infidelity play a role in what makes you angry?

There is no "score" for this self-test, no number of daily anger episodes that is permissible or not. The anger notebook will simply yield clues that can help confirm your suspicions that you may be suffering from chronic anger and help you uncover possible causes.

If you decide that you have a problem with chronic anger, some short-term therapy might help you bring your anger response under control. It is possible that the therapist you choose might ask you to take the Minnesota Multiphasic Personality Inventory we mentioned above, or another personality test, as a way to help determine how acute your anger might be, and how dangerous it has become in your health, life, and relationships.

SELF-CURES FOR ANGER

It is also possible that, through some or all of the above exercises and explorations, you may determine that you have a less acute problem with anger. Perhaps you become excessively angry at times, but it is only an occasional problem. If that is the case, here are some preventative steps to bring the problem under control before it lapses into patterns of jealousy or wreaks other harm:

- Talk openly with your spouse or partner about the anger-related problems you are experiencing. In a caring relationship where you enjoy a good level of communication, airing the problem can serve as the most effective and healing approach.

- Speak with a trusted friend or confidant about your anger. Talk about what makes you angry and invite suggestions and comments.

IDENTIFYING YOUR ANGER "TRIGGERS"

It can also prove helpful to identify your specific anger "triggers" and work to loosen their ability to unsettle you. For example, one man was becoming very irate at least three times a week because his wife and children took so long to get ready to leave the house that they were consistently late to appointments.

CYNICISM IS BAD FOR YOU

In the early 1990s, Karen A. Matthews, Ph.D., a professor of psychiatry, psychology, and epidemiology at the University of Pittsburgh, studied the hostility levels of 374 white and African-American men between the ages of eighteen and thirty. She conducted a second study of the participants a decade later to check their coronary arteries for signs of calcification, an early sign of atherosclerosis, and reported her findings in the *Journal of the American Medical Association*.

The results were striking. Participants who scored above the median on the hostility assessment were twice as likely to have coronary calcification as those scoring below the median.

Source: *Journal of the American Medical Association*, vol. 283, no. 19 (2000)

We also know a married woman who was angered every day upon arriving home from work when she found that her husband had left a pile of dirty dishes in the sink for her to wash. Such problems can often be defused by communicating about the problem and agreeing on corrective action you and/or your partner can take.

More times than we like to admit, we are participants in the problem that is "setting us off" and making us angry. It can therefore be helpful to accept some of the blame for the situation that is causing our anger and take a role in defining, and taking, corrective action.

The man we describe above who is angry because his family is slow to leave the house, for instance, can decide that he will tell his family that if they want to be late for every appointment, that is their decision and he will not allow the problem to upset him anymore. The woman who faces the dirty dishes can decide that she will tell her husband that it would be considered as a sign of respect by her if he would clean up after himself so she does not have to come back to a dirty home.

Even low-level chronic anger can function like a "ticking time bomb" within a relationship, waiting to erupt into jealousy. Confronting and alleviating the problem are necessary steps to take to insulate your relationship from the destructive power of anger. The Othello response, we know, often follows close behind.

CHAPTER 10
TRUST AS A SOLID FOUNDATION FOR YOUR RELATIONSHIP

Romeo: Lady, by yonder blessed moon I vow,
That tips with silver all these fruit-tree tops—
Juliet: O, swear not by the moon, th'inconstant moon,
That monthly changes in her circled orb,
Lest that thy love prove likewise variable.
Romeo: What shall I swear by?
Juliet: Do not swear at all;
Or, if thou wilt, swear by thy gracious self,
Which is the god of my idolatry,
And I'll believe thee.

—*Romeo and Juliet*, Act II, Scene 2

WHEN A LOVING RELATIONSHIP IS stable, secure, and free from jealousy, mutual trust is often the underlying cause. When trust is absent, its lack often reveals itself in a number of ways, as these case studies show:

■ "I travel a lot on business," Steve tells us. "When I am away, my wife calls often. I think it is really to check up on me. I have been forced to designate certain activities as permissible, such as going to the movies alone, dining alone, or sitting in my hotel room watching movies. Other activities are decidedly off-limits, such as meeting colleagues in a hotel bar for a late-night drink or even going to a play with a group of people. It is just easier to play by the rules than to risk upsetting my wife. When some kind of disruption has taken place in this area, it takes a lot of work to make her feel happy again."

■ "My mother was never allowed to drive," Mary tells us. "My dad said he was trying to keep her from having an accident, but he simply wanted to be in control of what she did at all times."

■ "Last year an old friend of mine, recently divorced, invited my wife and me to join him for dinner," Jon recalls. "He brought along a date, just someone he was seeing, and they behaved very affectionately and flirtatiously, like a couple of teenagers on a date. Afterward, my wife was very upset. After a few days, she told me that she was unable to set aside the idea that I, too, was about to leave her and start a relationship with another woman. She said we had become 'set in our ways,' that our relationship was 'tired' and it took a long time to get everything calm again."

TRUST AS A BUFFER AGAINST THE OTHELLO RESPONSE

When trust is present, it can serve as a protection against such incursions of the Othello response, as shown in this story from a man named Dave: "Last year, a friend called to tell me that he had just seen my wife having lunch with a well-dressed man in a restaurant. I think he believed that he was calling me with some big piece of news. My wife is a successful entrepreneur and often entertains customers over a meal. I explained that to him and really did not think about it after that. I expect he was projecting onto our relationship the way he would feel if he learned that his wife was having a quiet lunch with another man. I trust my wife, and she trusts me."

BUILDING TRUST

So we see that trust can determine whether or not a relationship is vulnerable to the onset of obsessive jealousy. What is this hard-to-define yet invaluable asset known as trust?

One dictionary defines it as "an assured reliance on the integrity and truth and friendship of a person."

That is a good operative definition. Certainly, the word *assured* conveys a strong sense of comfort and assurance. When you feel assured in your relationship, you don't just *believe* that your partner has integrity and trustworthiness; you are completely convinced of it. Trust lies at a deep level of your consciousness.

In a love relationship, trust means that you can rely on your spouse, your friend, your loved one, your partner. You believe

WHEN TRUST IS LACKING

Some people live together but don't know the details of each other's lives. A man who came to see author Ken Ruge for counseling didn't even know the name of the family cat, although that pet had lived with them for five years. Another man didn't know what his wife did at work. She just went away and came back and they didn't ever talk about it.

Little wonder that these couples were experiencing difficulties. Simple familiarity is a basic foundation in building trust. It is often in secret areas where no knowledge is shared that doubts and uncertainties breed and take hold.

in that other person and know that he or she will be there for you and has your best interests at heart. You know he or she will care for you. You can rely on it. You are enjoying a committed relationship or marriage as it ought to be.

Where does trust come from? When does it begin? It does not automatically drop down onto a relationship the moment the partners say, "I love you," or exchange rings, marriage vows, or a promise to be faithful to each other. Much as we like to believe in the curative power of romance, trust takes time. If it is to flourish and grow, there needs to be a deep, cultivated sense of familiarity with another person. Clearly, he or she needs to feel the same level of trust in you too. Trust is not a one-sided equation. It needs to be in balance or some disruption inevitably occurs.

Erik Erikson, the famous developmental psychologist, spent a great deal of time studying the dynamics of trust. He observed that a basic dialectic, consisting of *trust* vs. *mistrust*, was operative in infants very early on. In fact, from birth to age two, much of a baby's experiential world revolves around issues of trust and mistrust.

In the early parent/child relationship, trust operates as the operative currency. The baby's sense of being able to trust its parents or caregivers is of paramount importance. Will that infant be held, not dropped? Will it receive food? Will its diapers be changed? Will parents intervene if that baby becomes upset, needs to be burped, or cannot fall asleep? As the child grows toward adolescence, will the caretakers or parents help as the child falls victim to all the emotional upsets that are literally "infantile" from an adult point of view, yet highly threatening for a child?

Through daily interactions, a sense of trust gradually

evolves. Through it, a child builds the ability to have faith in another person—the capability to trust. When trust is not there, or a parent is untrustworthy, problems surrounding the issue of trust often arise in adult life.

For example, children who had an unreliable parent often experience relational problems in adolescence, teenage years, or on into adulthood. Often, they tend to become attracted to partners who are untrustworthy. They stand a good chance of becoming adults who are not themselves trustworthy, or who have difficulty placing trust in another person. At other times, they may become excessively possessive of their partners. In such cases, that early childhood development of trust might have been impaired in some way.

John's Story

Consider John, a man who even in his adult life was wrestling with issues from his parents' marriage. In his childhood, he lived in a household where both his parents had emotions that were often volatile. They argued a lot, especially on weekends. Then when Monday came, the disagreements seemed to be set aside, and life returned to "normal." When John grew up and married, he vowed never to behave in such damaging ways. But very soon, months into his marriage in fact, he and his wife began to argue. Realizing that these patterns must have "come from somewhere," John and his wife saw a marital therapist and began to explore whether arguing was a common occurrence in the families of John or his wife. By pursuing this path of inquiry, they were both able to understand the problem and take steps to bring it under control.

At this point you may be thinking, "This is interesting. I

now realize that my parents were unreliable and that I might be placing some unnecessary burdens on my relationship, such as not being able to trust my partner. That is good to know, but what am I supposed to do to stop thinking and acting this way?"

That is an important question to ask, but you would do well to remember that just by asking it, you are already seeking some wisdom and insight about how to deal with the trust that was lacking in your early years. When you stop to consider your parents' trustworthiness or lack thereof, you will be led to ask a stream of other questions. These might suggest positive steps that can help heal or inoculate your relationship from trust-related problems, such as feelings of obsessive jealousy or overdependence on a partner.

Some advice follows. Depending on the nature of your love relationship, it might or might not apply to you. We'd urge you to read it through with patience, point by point, since some insights might help you uncover and understand trust-related issues in your relationship.

If trust was lacking in your family of origin—if a parent was unreliable, if people could not be counted upon:

- It may be important for you to engage in relationships with individuals who grew up in loving, trust-filled families. When we pick our spouses, we don't often interview their parents. Perhaps we should. The families we come from are the basic foundation from which trust evolves. (It can be worthwhile to consider the psychodynamics of marital choice and how we decide who we will eventually forge loving bonds with or marry.)

■ You might need to confront the fact that your own ability to trust might be impaired to a greater or lesser degree. Perhaps you are someone who tends to doubt trustworthiness, even in partners who are reliable and dependable.

■ You might question whether you tend to be attracted to unreliable, unstable partners. After all, instability was part of your family system when growing up and you might tend to gravitate toward people who are also unsteady. If you have been taught to see unreliability as a normal part of loving relationships, you may have unconsciously been attracted to unstable partners.

If trust was lacking in your partner's family of origin—if a parent was unreliable, if people could not be counted upon:

■ You may have been "placed on a pedestal" in your relationship, elevated to the status of someone who is seen as wonderful and beyond fault because you will never betray your partner or engage in the kind of intrigues he or she suffered at home while growing up. It is nice to be honored for your positive traits, but being idolized carries clear risks. Because of the elevated expectations directed your way, even small transgressions on your part can lead you to take a tumble in the eyes of an overappreciative partner.

■ Be aware that he or she may impute unreliability or even unfaithfulness to you, even when that is not reality-based or fair. After all, such vicissitudes were seen as a normal part of his or her family system and may become projected upon you as a result. His or her ability to fully trust you may be impaired, a situation that may require work and joint exploration.

If Your Parents Avoided Conflict

Our parents' arguing and instability are not the only problems that can lead to the eruption of jealousy in our adult relationships. Perhaps you grew up in a household where your parents never fought, but avoided conflict at all costs. They were gridlocked, they didn't talk about problems, and perhaps they led what we might call "parallel lives," where they lived and slept together but never achieved a deep level of intimacy. If that was the case, you too may have a somewhat off-center image of what a close relationship ought to be—very civil, but essentially unconnected. Such relationships appear to function suitably for some couples, and sometimes they endure for extended periods of time. But usually they do not. In our current culture where divorce is an option that is more often exercised, people are less likely to soldier on indefinitely in unrewarding, gridlocked relationships.

The ideal, if one exists in loving relationships, is to forge a vibrant relationship where you and your partner are closely connected, where you can discuss and resolve conflicts appropriately. Often, that means understanding the baggage you are carrying from your own early years, and naming those problems and bringing them to the conscious level, so you can avoid falling victim yourself.

Arriving at this heightened level of awareness need not be a threatening process. The woman in one marriage, for example, began to use humor to remind her husband when he was beginning to act like his own father. "You're becoming Carl again!" she would say. With humor, they could catch the pattern, change it, and finally loosen its disruptive power over them.

BUILDING A FOUNDATION OF FAMILIARITY

Whatever your expectations and "baggage" surrounding the issue of trust, how can you build more of it into your relationship with your spouse or partner?

One important first step is to cultivate a sense of genuine familiarity with the person you love. Too often, we believe that circumstances will work on our behalf in this area. After all, you made a commitment. Maybe you even got married or you are living together, sharing your bed, board, and daily routines. Perhaps you have children and make joint decisions about related issues. Maybe you have a joint banking account.

Don't such things do the work for you, laying a strong foundation for trust? Yes, but unfortunately, they are not always enough. Let's take a closer look at some of the building blocks of familiarity:

- *Spending simple time together.* Many of us have seen promising relationships founder because both partners are simply too occupied with other pursuits to make enough time for each other. In addition to the quantity of time, we need to remember that *quality* of time is an important consideration too. There are different kinds of time together. There is time sleeping together, time watching television, time being tired, or time driving to the train. And then there is time together that is of another order entirely: time talking about your personal hopes, aspirations for children, beliefs, fears of the unknown, concern for your partner's health and happiness. The term *quality time* has become overused and hackneyed today. Though overused, it might still be the best way to describe the kind of shared experience that builds an enduring sense of closeness and trust. (Perhaps *dedicated time* comes closer.) Without such an investment of simple time, trust can be hard to find. Because of what the author Stephen Covey calls our "busy/tired culture" where constant demands are placed on us, it is important to make a commitment to quality time. That may mean scheduling a weekly night out, planning romantic weekends—devoting time to keep focused on your relationship.

■ *Paying attention to each other, with concern.* Do you know your partner with what might be called "ongoing familiarity"? Do you know what he or she did yesterday and today at work? There were meetings at work, but what were they about? With whom does he or she spend the working day? Do you know anything about your partner's boss and colleagues, or are they unknown to you? Do you know where he or she buys a morning cup of coffee, spends lunch hours? And do you share such information about yourself?

■ *Being aware of the biggest challenges and issues your partner is currently facing.* Looking ahead, do you know the most important life issues your "other" will be facing today, tomorrow, and next week?

■ *Keeping in touch with fears, anxieties, and ambitions.* Who are his or her "enemies" and friends? Why? What is his or her level of healthy self-esteem? How much frustration, sadness, or anger is part of his or her daily experience? What does he or she dream for in life? What are the biggest ambitions and goals? How can you provide support where it is most needed and help uphold and support those dreams?

■ *Understanding your partner's history.* Did he or she have a favorite uncle, interesting cousins, a special relationship with a parent? Were there certain childhood events that were especially happy or especially sad? What problems have been faced and overcome?

To summarize, it is important to understand your partner deeply. You need to know your partner's fears, quirks, vulnerabilities, "hot buttons."

These are some of the factors that can help build a sense of ongoing familiarity, which is a foundation of trust. If you dedicate yourself to building a relationship on this deeper, more intimate level, you are less likely to end up living what might be called "parallel lives," which is a kind of stasis in which both partners are together, but living separately. When we fail to connect on a deeper, more rewarding level, we not only feel dissatisfied in our relationships. We also invite in a level of estrangement that can lead to "transgressions," jealousy, and other manifestations of the Othello response.

FOSTERING RESPECT

Along with familiarity, respect is another important building block in trust. Respect can be defined in different ways, but it can be taken to embody some or all of the following aspects:

■ *An appreciation for your partner's special assets.* He or she may be honest, accomplished, intelligent, a good listener, a loving parent—and the list could go on. To nurture a sense of respect, it is a good idea to bring these assets to the conscious level and become aware of them. Often, stopping to enumerate your partner's worth can lead not only to a greater appreciation, but to a deeper understanding of your relationship too.

■ A *clear idea of why your partner's special qualities are important to you.* This is a kind of meeting point—the place where your needs are met by the person you love. And clearly it is a process that works both ways, with you meeting your partner's needs too. Perhaps you have a special need for physical affection, and he or she meets that need magnificently. Or vice versa. Or perhaps you place your children at the center of your life and your partner is just as devoted to them as you are. Again, bringing these points of connection to the conscious level, and communicating about them, strengthens trust.

Sometimes it helps to understand that your partner's strengths are important for reasons that are rooted in your own childhood, family background, or personal past. If your father or mother, or previous lovers or partners, were not caring or loving in their relations with you, a partner's capacity for physical affection might take on extra importance for you. It is one of your special needs. Similarly, if your mother or father brought specific disruptions to your young life—alcoholism, a lack of involvement, abuse, or philandering—the assurance that your partner does not share those negative traits can help establish his or her particular value to you.

Often, frictions arise concerning issues of work. Perhaps

one partner invests more of him- or herself in work or career than the other, or one member of a relationship becomes frustrated with the other person's lack of drive in this area. Often, we define such roles and expectations based on the familial models we grew up with. If we grew up with a workaholic parent, for example, we are likely to become workaholics ourselves. If we are partnered with such a workaholic and are not workaholics ourselves, we can be at a loss to understand where the driven, "alien" behavior originated.

It can be a worthwhile exercise to initiate a discussion of your needs where such frictions crop up, and to explain how your partner is doing in meeting them. If your partner is sympathetic and meets your needs, maybe you could say how you admire him or her, and explain why. Bringing these issues into discussion might feel awkward at first, but it can allow a sense of fondness and admiration into your relationship.

A Sense of Beholding and Mutual Respect

Beholding is a word we don't use much today. It comes from the Christian spiritual tradition, and means seeing into the soul of another person on a deep level. When we behold others in this sense, we do more than just look at them. We look deeply into them and know who they are at their depth.

Even when couples do not realize they are "beholding" as such, many discover and benefit from a spiritual subtext, feeling that their relationship or their marriage was ordained by some higher power. They feel that there was, or is, some reason why they came together, perhaps a special reason they met.

In some couples, people even see their partners as "teachers" who are there to help them evolve and flourish in important ways. They value the special qualities that their partners possess. We see this often in the early stages of loving relationships, when a sudden exchange of interests usually takes place. Perhaps one partner loves great art and opens up the world of museums and galleries to a new partner who, in turn, shares knowledge of skiing, travel, or some other interesting pursuit. When this exchange of knowledge and this opening of new horizons is maintained long-term in a relationship, a special level of respect and esteem can result. Often, it is allowed to dwindle away.

As a relationship matures, there is a chance for tolerance to grow and a genuine exchange to happen. A committed relationship is one of the few places where we are able to give and get honest feedback on who we are and how we are. Thus a loving, mature relationship can become a crucible for growth.

Yet if you stop to take stock of your partner's special assets and abilities, you will find many. Perhaps your partner possesses a sense of integrity, an ability to open up new horizons, or a just a sense of beauty or the ability to use language well. Such appreciation, brought again to the conscious level, adds depth and trust to a relationship.

Learning to Pay Attention

Another building block beneath trust appears to be so obvious that it may seem puzzling that we mention it here at all. It is simply the importance of paying attention to your partner. Simple and self-evident though it may be, it is surprising that so few people engage in it.

Paying attention means listening to what the other person is saying, then acknowledging what has been said and responding. It also means enjoying a relationship in which you can talk and expect to be heard.

You have doubtless known couples who have been in

trouble. If you stop to recall their interactions during troubled times, you will doubtless recall that the people in those relationships were not paying much attention to each other. Yet even in relationships that seem stable and sound, it is remarkable how often one member of a couple will turn away and miss what is said by the partner, or drop the ball and fail to respond. If this disruptive communication process is allowed to continue and become habitual, the result can be an erosion in the quality of the relationship—again, a "parallel" relationship where two people live separate lives together without truly connecting.

It is all too easy to understand why people in our culture fail to accord deep attention to one another. We are so busy. We are centered on work, children, paying bills. One effective antidote to all those preoccupations is to actively schedule uninterrupted time with your partner. That might mean simply having a lunch together at a coffee shop while the kids are in school, or having a quiet dinner together, or even taking a drive in your car with no one but your partner present.

Spending undistracted time together on a regular basis affords a foundation for reconnecting and paying attention to what is going on in your partner's life. It is an active way to say, *I appreciate you, I honor you by listening to you, and I want to continue to know who you are as a person.* The deepening of commitment that follows these simple acts can be surprisingly profound.

EXERCISES FOR BUILDING TRUST IN YOUR MARRIAGE OR RELATIONSHIP

A common misconception holds that trust arises as a by-product of the good things that exist within a relationship. If you are kind and respectful of your partner, trust will grow.

For example, if a partner brings constancy and reliability to the relationship over time.

That may be true, but trust is also something that can be actively encouraged and cultivated in a relationship. Here are some exercises we would encourage you to try:

- *Openly share admiration for each other.* As the couple enjoys private time alone, one partner describes the qualities that he or she most appreciates and admires in the other partner. The person who is being appreciated must listen quietly and carefully. Then, roles are reversed and the exercise is repeated. This is not easy! It is often hard for a person to hear positive things about him- or herself. It is sometimes embarrassing or difficult. But once the exercise is over, it is often amazing to see what happens. Often, both partners discover that they have added a new and valuable building block to the foundation of their relationship. Both people reach a new understanding about what the other person respects, appreciates, and admires. To actually state these things, which might have been on the minds of both partners for some time, leads to increased levels of respect, admiration, and fondness.

- *Take a walk up a mountain together and talk about how you are doing in the pursuit of your individual dreams.* First, one person gets to talk about his or her dreams and how well they are being achieved. Then roles are reversed. (You might get to talk about your dreams on the way up the mountain, and your partner on the way down.) The idea of focusing on our personal dreams and how we are doing on them, and the complementary process of being supported by a partner, breeds deep trust. According to marital researcher John Gottman, supporting individual dreams is an important contributor to the stability of marriages and relationships.

■ *The romantic weekend—or just a night out.* Find a way to enjoy one within your budget. If you have kids, arrange for child care. Spend some dedicated time together in a place that is not where you usually find yourselves. The goal is not to be limited in your time together or confined to talking about logistics—who paid what bills, who is chauffeuring the kids where, etc. You are actually looking at each other and talking.

■ *Take a drive together alone.* Moving in a car together can be a metaphor for moving ahead together. Or read a good book to each other. Or listen to a book on tape or CD.

■ *Seek a powerful emotional experience that moves both you and your partner.* If you love classical music, go to a performance by an artist you both love. Or if you are religious, attend services together. It could even be a movie! It could be a verbal experience, or a nonverbal one. Sharing an experience that "makes the hair stand up on the back of your necks" can be a powerful reconnector.

■ *Seek a shared experience in a context that reanchors you with the roots of your early relationship.* It might be revisiting the place where you were married, or where you first fell in love. Or perhaps engaging in some activity that dates from your early years together. This kind of shared refreshing activity can remind both you and your partner of why you are together—and why you ought to be together.

CHAPTER 11
MAKE UP OR BREAK UP: THE POWER OF HEALING OUR RELATIONSHIPS

We had both been silent a long time,
But then speech came suddenly back to us.
The angels, who fly down from heaven,
Brought peace again after all our strife . . .
The angels of love came during the night
And brought peace to my heart.

>   — "Wir haben beide lange Zeit geschwiegen,"
>   by the German poet Paul Heyse (1830–1914),
>   trans. Barry Lenson

IT HAS OFTEN BEEN said that disagreements are part of being in love. By and large, that is true. Yet after you and your partner have a conflict or a quarrel, it is very important that you find a way to make up. Healing the relationship in this way demonstrates that you and your partner are fundamentally in a good place together. A disruption has occurred, but things remain sound and well supported by goodwill and mutual support.

Failure to mend a relationship after rifts, according to

John Gottman and other leading marital researchers, is a very strong predictor of divorce and relationship failure. When conflicts are allowed to fester or to disperse gradually over time, the result is most often erosion of the relationship. Over time, failure to make up often leads one or both partners to seek a "happier place" outside their relationship. That happier place could be a simple escape or something more destructive:

■ Establishing a close, special relationship with someone other than the partner

■ Going down to the corner bar to spend every evening drinking with friends, like Norm on *Cheers*

■ Watching sports on television for hours and hours

■ Working long hours to escape an uncomfortable relationship at home

■ Beginning a hobby that places extreme demands on time, like training for a marathon or spending all weekend, every weekend, working on the Corvette in the garage

■ Engaging in a "casual" or short-term affair

GRADUAL EROSION

A man named Mark saw just such a pattern evolving in the two years he was living with his lover, Marshall. When he and Marshall would argue or disagree, they would never apologize or attempt to "heal" the bad feelings that had occurred. Instead, they just got up the next day, behaved in an outwardly peaceful way, got dressed, and went off to their jobs. They believed that such patterns were a normal, expected part of the kind of relationship they were engaged in. But inside, things were beginning to boil. A growing sense of alienation and estrangement took hold, finally ending the relationship when both men found themselves longing for, and finally moving into, other relationships. Jealous arguments were their parting shots. Had some regular attempts at postdisagreement healing begun early in the relationship, they might have preserved and deepened it over time.

THE DECEPTIVE POWER OF ARGUING

It is remarkable how pervasive arguing and disruptions can become before people realize that something is fundamentally askew in their relationships. One couple, for example, came to see Ken Ruge, saying simply that they wanted to "communicate better." After some discussion, it became clear that they were arguing a lot. How many fights were they having? Oh, only about three a month. How long did the battles last? Oh, usually about seven days, during which time they did not speak to each other. You can do the math on this for yourself: they were arguing about 75 percent of the time.

Such patterns, not surprisingly, are reliable predictors of the demise of relationships and divorce.

Making a commitment to reconnect and make up after rifts is an important way to say that you and your partner had a conflict, yes, but that you are still in a fundamentally good, secure place in your relationship. The difficulties were temporary. They did not signal that you were no longer in love, nor did they become the seeds of growing alienation from each other.

FEET FIRST: DEATH AS AN EXTREME EXIT STRATEGY

Some people continue to be steadfastly loyal to their marriages and relationships, even when it is clear that the relationship is not working. They refuse to accept the idea that sometimes people really do need to break up and get away from each other. For reasons that might come from childhood, they insist upon riding things out to the end, "no matter what," without taking any real steps to make things better.

Some people actually die to get out of their relationships, though they surely do not view what they do in that way. This was the case with our friend Paul's mother. She was a woman from a rigid Scandinavian background, and she would *never* leave her marriage. She just kept soldiering along, often in great unhappiness, until her health began to suffer and she finally went into decline and died.

Many unhealthy variations on this pattern emerge when people decide to remain in unhealthy relationships without being able to make improvements. Some people gain large amounts of weight in order to make themselves unattractive to their partners—in effect, to "hide" both from them and from other possible sexual partners too. Other people smoke, drink alcohol, or engage in other unhealthy vices that might well be viewed as an attempt at long-term suicide to escape the relationship.

"Feet first" is not the only way to exit a relationship. Healthier possibilities exist.

SEEKING TO HEAL

What keeps relationships working—and often working *well*—is that both partners show a willingness to find effective ways to bring disruptions to resolution and abbreviate them so that they lose their power to do permanent harm. In other words, they *make up*.

The making up itself can be an apology. It could be compassionately admitting that you played some part in the conflict. It could be apologizing for certain language you used or things you said. Or it could be as simple as making a joke that breaks the tension.

One couple we know, for example, has a nearly comic ritual for signaling that a conflict has ended. The woman in the relationship gently socks her husband in his arm. She does so affectionately and laughingly and since her husband is a bulked-up weight lifter, she cannot possibly do any real harm. This interaction is actually affectionate, and a nice thing to witness. She socks him, they both laugh, and then they move on because they know the emotional upset has been released.

We are not suggesting hitting as a way to resolve conflict. In your relationship, the tension-breaker could be a hug or kiss. It could be reaching out and squeezing your partner's hand. Such small gestures can communicate the news that your relationship is not perfect, but that you are feeling good about being in it anyway. You're making a gesture that says, "We are fundamentally solid, sailing along on an even keel."

This kind of ritualistic healing, though it appears casual, offers a highly effective way to insulate your relationship against the Othello response and other relational problems in general. Healing is cumulative, and over time it makes a difference.

IAGO AS PROTAGONIST

As the composer Giuseppe Verdi and the playwright Arrigo Boito were creating their operatic version of *Othello,* they decided for a time to change the name of their new opera to *Iago.* For these two giants of the Italian theater, Iago was more interesting than Othello and by far the most compelling and complex character in the play. Only at the end of their collaboration did Verdi and Boito change their plans and name their new opera *Otello.*

THE POWER OF ADMITTING YOU WERE WRONG

Of the many healing gestures available to us, admitting personal wrongdoing may well be the most powerful. It also comes with great difficulty for so many of us. Consider these words that underscore so clearly our personal need to be "right" in our loving relationships:

- "I know I was wrong to use such harsh words with my girlfriend when we had an argument last week," a man name Sid tells us, "yet I was right to say what I said. I have no intention of taking back anything!"

- "I went out to lunch with my tennis instructor," a married woman named Sheila admits, "and then we went to his apartment and had sex. I'm married, but I had a right to do that because my husband is so involved with his career that he cannot give me the affection I need. Why should I tell him about it? My husband cut me off long ago. He doesn't even need to know."

- "I know I spend all my time going to sporting events with my buddies," Jack tells us, "but my wife has gotten to be such a drag. Every time I show up, she wants me to fix something around the house. I have to have some fun."

- "I know I've been looking at some pretty questionable things on the Internet," Sally says, "visiting pornographic chat rooms and so on. But it's not like I'm having real sex with anybody but my boyfriend. Lots of other people are doing it too."

Admitting personal wrongdoing, or even admitting that we

had intention to do something wrong, can be an important step in both preserving our primary love relationships and making sure that the Othello response does not contaminate us. Admitting personal wrong is not often easy, but the results can be worthwhile if your loving relationship is worth protecting and preserving.

Michael and Virginia

This case study of a married couple, Michael and Virginia, offers ample evidence of the curative power of admitting personal guilt. Let's start at the beginning. Both of them had models for marital instability in their families while they were growing up. Michael's mother was very emotional and effusive, a former classical musician who overstepped appropriate parental guidelines and spoke openly with Michael about her personal and sexual dissatisfaction with Michael's father, who was a reserved and withdrawn executive. Perhaps because her husband was so unavailable emotionally, she ended up expressing her frustration to Michael in unfit ways.

Virginia's family seemed outwardly less volatile than Michael's. Her mother was a strong, domineering figure. Her father was passive and apparently kind. They were loyal to each other, but outwardly reserved and unaffectionate. They were living the kind of unconnected "parallel lives" we discussed earlier in this chapter: together, but not deeply connected. As a result, Virginia did not harbor particularly high expectations for marriage in general. She simply wanted a faithful man who would support her quietly and steadily, without making excessive emotional demands.

Virginia's particular needs for calm stability were not met in relationships she had engaged in before she met Michael.

Several of her earlier lovers were unfaithful to her, causing her to angrily terminate the relationships at once and search for someone who would be more dependable. When Virginia met Michael, Virginia was certain that she had found a man who would remain loyal to her—a consideration that was of paramount importance to her.

Things remained stable and satisfactory for six years, while the couple lived contentedly in the suburbs outside Boston. Then Michael, a successful banker, got transferred to San Francisco. Because of Virginia's own career, she remained in Boston while Michael rented an apartment near his new job. They envisioned that their professional separation would last for a year or two, then Michael would be transferred back home and things would become normal again.

The distance immediately caused some problems. Without the daily familiarity of simply "being there" for each other, they began to lose track of each other. Michael soon found that he was frustrated because his personal and sexual needs were not being met in the new situation. Perhaps because of the high importance that his effusive mother had attached to getting her personal and sexual "due" from her own partner, Michael lived with an expectation that sexual gratification was of paramount importance in his life. He greatly enjoyed being attractive to women. Across the continent, Virginia was living in a way that was consistent with her own familial expectations. She felt sure that, because of marriage, both of them had agreed to remain faithful until they could be together again. She was living fairly contentedly at home. For her, the operative value in marriage was not to get your personal needs met, but rather to endure and remain committed to a relationship.

In a business meeting one day, Michael met Jeanne, a young graphic designer who had come in to consult on a project. He was immediately attracted to her. She was also an amateur singer and she invited him to attend a concert given by her choral group, which he attended. That led to a luncheon date, followed by several dinner dates. The level of physical affection between Michael and Jeanne was increasing. On the night Jeanne invited him to her apartment for dinner, it escalated to the point of kissing and fondling, though it stopped short of sexual relations.

At this point, something "clicked" for Michael. He realized that he was complimented and excited by the growing relationship with Jeanne, but that his marriage was ultimately much more important than his immediate need to feel attractive or have sex. He resolved that he did not want his relationship with Jeanne to go any farther. Instead, he wanted to revitalize and revive his relationship with Virginia, to make his essentially sound marriage work.

In order to do that, he realized he would have to pursue a rather difficult course. To his credit, he decided to do something dangerous and potentially destabilizing to his marriage. Instead of hiding what had nearly happened, he decided to tell Virginia that he had nearly started an affair with another woman, but had decided not to do so because his marriage meant so much to him.

So when Michael and Virginia were next together, he did just that. He explained that he felt that their marriage was not working, that he had been tempted to begin an affair with another woman, but that he had not done so. He said he wanted them to talk and find a way that they could make their marriage more sound and happy. He believed that his full admission would demonstrate his commitment and honesty to Virginia, yet his statements did not immediately cause the beneficial response he was hoping for. Virginia blew up and became nearly hysterical, perhaps because Michael had broken one of the ground rules she thought they both had understood and accepted—simple fidelity. Virginia felt betrayed by him because he hadn't told her about his relationship with Jeanne sooner. For days, she was convinced their marriage could not be healed.

Yet over time, they were able to break the cycle of defensiveness that infects relationships at such times: the tendency to say, "I was wrong to do what I did, but you were also wrong when you . . ." Virginia also began to admit some personal culpability for the erosion that had infected their relationship. Then the clouds began to clear and they initiated discussions about productive steps they could take to heal their relationship. One day in a restaurant they made a list of grievances and issues that troubled them about their marriage. They began to make some changes, restructuring their careers so they could make more time to be together. As a result, their sexual relationship became revitalized. They even made plans to renew their marriage vows in the same setting where they were married.

It is possible that all these changes could have come about if Michael had made a "half confession" about his incipient affair, or concealed it entirely. But probably not. The ability to admit wrongdoing and feed it back into the warp and weave of a loving relationship, in this case at least, worked as a catalyst for needed change and restoration. As a result of this attempt at healing, trust returned. They were even able to grant each other a degree of healthy autonomy again.

Respecting autonomy means we trust our partners enough to let them pursue their own interests—even when we are not part of them. It means lending them moral support, even though we may not share their particular passions. Even in the closest relationships, we need time to follow our own pursuits, enjoy our own space and privacy, and even to be alone.

This is the paradoxical nature of love and trust. We need our relationships. We need our partners. Yet unless we also remain true to ourselves, we take away half of what makes a relationship work.

It would be unrealistic to expect that any partnership or marriage would be free from its difficult periods and specific incidents that test the commitment of both partners to be together. Disruptions are part of any relationship. When two complex people come together, it would be unrealistic to expect anything else.

What determines the durability and success of the relationship is not the absence of such events, but rather the couple's ability to recover and heal after disruptions have occurred. Such healing is not a passive activity. It requires both partners to communicate, setting aside defensiveness and ego-feeding notions of who is right and who is wrong. Its success often hinges on good humor and an underlying level of trust.

Yet it is worth all the effort and difficulty. The result is a relationship that has been tested in the "fire of adversity" and emerged strengthened and renewed. In the end, a couple's ability to heal is the greatest predictor of the ongoing success of their relationship.

CHAPTER 12
GUILT, FEAR, AND FORGIVENESS

Othello: Why, what art thou?

Desdemona: Your wife, my lord; your true

And loyal wife.

Othello: Come, swear it, damn thyself

Lest, being like one of heaven, the devils themselves

Should fear to seize thee: therefore be double damn'd:

Swear thou art honest.

Desdemona: Heaven doth truly know it.

Othello: Heaven truly knows that thou art false as hell.

—*Othello*, Act IV, Scene 2

JEALOUSY AND GUILT ARE closely intertwined. Like the words of the old song "Love and Marriage," it seems you can't have one without the other. To be sure, if one partner in a relationship has had an affair, guilt often becomes a pressing issue that needs to be discussed and explored by both partners if the relationship is to be preserved. Yet guilt doesn't only appear when an actual infidelity has occurred. It is surprising to note that in many ways, large and small, small parcels of guilt are part of any relationship. Perhaps you're guilty because you bought a small present for your partner's birthday instead of the one you really wanted to buy. Or in a social context, maybe you told a little lie to break off a lunch date with a friend. Or perhaps you had a party in your home and didn't invite certain friends, and now you are feeling guilty about that. Guilt seems to be part of human interaction.

Yet is guilt all bad? Not necessarily, although we most often think of it as a negative force that embodies concepts of remorse, blame, regret, and even failure. Guilt can be healthy

IAGO AS THE EMBODIMENT OF PURE EVIL

Othello and Desdemona are towering creations of Shakespeare's intellect. In contrast, Iago appears to emerge from somewhere else—from some elemental place of absolute evil. Harold Bloom, the Shakespearean critic, tells us that as Shakespeare wrote the play *Othello*, he continually reworked and refined. But in creating Iago, Shakespeare did hardly any rewriting at all.

It is as though Iago sprang onto the stage, fully formed from some place deep within Shakespeare. Surely Iago resides in that same place in all of us, a place of elemental evil. He leads us to doubt everything good, despise everything pure, and deny all that is good in our own hearts.

It is interesting to note that the full range of Iago's evil is possible only because he was once good. Just as people who become obsessively jealous were once true in their love for their partners, Iago has turned away from the good toward an alternate, dark world. There are many glimpses of Iago's former trustworthiness. In Act I, Scene 3, when Othello turns Desdemona over to Iago for safe transport to Cyprus, he praises Iago and calls Iago "a man of honesty and trust. To his conveyance I assign my wife."

In fact, it is Iago's track record of being trustworthy that makes it so easy for him to lead Othello into a new, false landscape from which he cannot emerge. Othello and other characters repeatedly call Iago "honest." ("I never knew a Florentine more kind and honest," Cassio says of him in Act III, Scene 1, even after Iago has all but brought him to ruin.)

too. Like many of life's uncomfortable emotions, it often directs our attention to areas of our lives that need "work" and where we have the most potential to make progress and grow. When guilt is used as an impetus to analyze and heal our relationship, guilt can sometimes help orient us:

■ At their monthly luncheons, Paulette and her circle of female friends often degenerated into what they humorously called "hubby bashing hour." Usually it started when one of her friends said something disparaging about her husband, then others chimed in. One month, Paulette surprised herself by saying rather vehemently that her "loser" husband had failed at three attempts to start his own business. She said some very unkind things, and felt guilty afterward. These feelings of remorse led her to conclude that she was not supporting her spouse sufficiently—either in his attempts at entrepreneurship or in her ability to honor him and hold him in esteem for his many positive traits

■ Carl liked to look at *Playboy* magazines and similar publications, but he didn't want his wife, Gina, to know. At first, he would buy a magazine, hide it for a few days while he looked at it, then secretly throw it away. Soon, he began to hide a few copies in the garage and other places where he was sure they would not be found. He engaged in a lot of self-justification around the issue of the materials he liked to read. ("After all, I'm not looking at the kind of horrible or deviant material I see on the newsstands," he told himself.) At the same time, he greatly respected Gina as a wonderful wife and mother. He began to worry that Gina would find his hidden cache of magazines. He began to feel guilty about what he was doing. He discarded the magazines. Although he didn't ever confess this "transgression" to his wife, he did resolve to honor her more and accord her the level of respect she really deserved.

Those stories are about people who somehow resolved to deal responsibly, and responsively, to feelings of guilt. There are less healthy ways to deal with guilt too. Often, guilt leads people who have "betrayed" their partners in some way to conceal what has happened, or simply to deny that anything happened. Some "straying" members of relationships go so far as to create secretive new shadow lives in which they continue to sustain one or more relationships in addition to their primary ones. The causes of such clandestine sexual activity are complex, but guilt and the desire to avoid blame are usually strong underlying motivations.

Paradoxically, when an infidelity has taken place, it is not only the "straying" partner who experiences guilt. The betrayed member of the relationship often feels guilty too, for having been unable to keep an infidelity from occurring.

What is guilt? Let's take a closer look.

THE HEALTHY SIDE OF GUILT

Guilt is never a happy emotion to experience, yet at its root, it usually functions in a healthy way by sending us warning signals that we have violated inner values or promises we have made to ourselves. Often, these are high personal standards, such as commitments to be faithful, honest, kind, or generous. Seen in this way, it becomes clear that guilt can serve as a positive impetus to keep us oriented toward our core values and the most important standards we have set for ourselves.

Guilt has a secondary function too. It helps us avoid making bad judgments that could endanger us mentally, and even physically:

- Consider Mary, a woman who has already been through the process of repairing a relationship with her husband after she had a brief affair with another man a few years ago. Now, whenever she meets a man and feels attracted to him, a flash of guilt reminds her how badly she hurt her husband and how much work it took to put things back together. Guilt sounds an alert when she is in a position to damage her relationship again.

- Or consider Sharon, a sixth grader who stopped herself just as she was about to do something her mom and dad said she shouldn't do: take a shortcut home from school by crossing some railroad tracks. As she was walking home one day with some friends, one of them suggested that they take the forbidden shortcut. Sharon first felt guilty because she was contemplating doing something her parents had asked her not to do. Then she remembered that there was a safety issue to be considered: the shortcut had been banned because it was dangerous! She took the longer way home more safely, thanks to a reminder sent up by guilt.

These stories illustrate that normal, healthy guilt can serve as an internal regulator that keeps our lives on track, safe and smooth. But we also know that guilt is not always so positive. In relation to the Othello response, guilt can run amok in several ways:

■ First, we can project our guilt onto our partners. Projection is our tendency to ascribe or attribute to the outer world what is happening in our own minds and inner selves. We end up blaming our partners for thoughts or fantasies that are actually in our own minds. At times, such projection becomes so intense that we virtually condemn everything about our partners by thinking, "I'm the good, guiltless one in this relationship!" or even, "I am all good, and my partner is all bad!" When our view of reality has become distorted to this point, an "exit strategy" is often at work. The guilt-directing partner is creating a negative scenario against his or her partner to be used as a justification for leaving the relationship.

Not all cases of projection are as pronounced or dramatic. Often, projection manifests itself in something as simple as saying, "I believe you are upset" when we are upset, or saying, "I sense you are bored in our relationship" when the boredom actually resides in us. Or saying, "You are not interested in sex anymore" when we are the parties who are losing that interest.

Our old friend guilt, again, is often the underlying cause of such patterns. We feel too guilty to openly say (even to ourselves) that we are bored, that we may want to be unfaithful, or that we are having thoughts that do not conform to the standards we want to uphold in our lives. To avoid shouldering the blame, we direct it toward our partners, with damaging consequences. This tendency can be especially acute in people who adhere to extremely rigid, moralistic religions and systems that dismiss all erotic tendencies as unthinkably off-limits and sinful.

■ Second, we suppress or repress our unacceptable desires. *Suppression* occurs when we harbor desires or needs that are so unacceptable to us that we guiltily attempt to conceal or deny them. The result can be an almost unbearable level of tension in our lives. Perhaps the most common and well-known instance of this can be seen in stories of emerging gay men and women whose homosexuality is in conflict with their religious beliefs or the "morals" put forth by their families or communities. For such people, the coming-out process can be especially painful and traumatic.

Bringing other repudiated desires into the open is often nearly as painful as that. In some cases, it is nearly impossible. It may be inconceivable for some of us to admit to our partners that we are experiencing sexual interest for individuals outside our partnerships. For so many of us, it is simply easier to delay talking about such issues. Sometimes it is even possible to put off those difficult conversations indefinitely. Better to avoid conflict than bring the issue out into the open, even if that means living unhappily for years and years.

REPRESSION

Repression is a very acute form of suppression that occurs when our ideas or desires are so completely unacceptable to us that they actually get shuttled into our subconscious. Such repressed problems and issues can be difficult to define or understand. Since they cannot generally be named, they often bubble to the surface of our lives in the form of violent thoughts and actions or the irrational jealousy of the Othello response:

- Becky, a student, developed an irrational crush on Keith, another student at her college. Because she had been brought up in a strictly religious family of fundamentalist Christians, she felt guilty about this infatuation because

Keith was "outside" her faith. In frustration, Becky began to date Peter, another young man who was from her own religious tradition and hence "acceptable" in the eyes of her parents. However, Becky soon began to act very cruelly and manipulatively toward Peter. In fact, she made him feel inadequate at all times by directing a constant stream of demands and shifting expectations at him. She was "acting out" her frustrations at not being free to approach Keith and other men whom she found attractive. At the same time, her strict set of family-imposed values made it difficult for her to understand why she was acting so erratically. Instead, she tried to make Peter feel worthless and upset.

■ Bill, who is now a well-adjusted man of sixty, reports that he underwent a period of extreme conflict until the age of thirty, surrounding the issues of his homosexuality. In high school, he kept his sexual orientation under wraps, as did many gay men of his generation because of prevailing anti-homosexual attitudes. In college, he continued to conceal his interest in other men and even went on to enter into a marriage that lasted only a few years, when his wife began a relationship with another man. Curiously, the fact that his wife was "guilty" of having an affair served as a mechanism for him to pass through the dissolution of his marriage without considering his homosexuality at the same time. Now, after a lengthy period of "coming out" and finding a social context where he feels supported, he is happy and on track. He now states that many of his youthful problems were caused, as he says, "by pushing my gay self down so hard and denying it that I was able at times to convince myself that it wasn't even there."

One result of suppression and repression is often some variety of projection, which we describe above. Since we are unable to deal with our own needs and desires and the guilt they foster in us, we pin the blame elsewhere. If our partner's affection is waning, some kind of infidelity is probably taking place. Surely, we cannot be to blame. Even if we are experiencing a desire to betray our partners, we tend to pin those desires on those we love.

IDEALIZATION AND GUILT: A DANGEROUS COMBINATION

Guilt is also triggered when we are unable to live up to the romanticized notions of love and marriage that pervade our culture. Even when we are wise enough to know that "happily ever after" only happens at the end of fairy tales and Disney cartoons, we are often surprised when our partners cannot fulfill all our emotional, sexual, and amorous needs.

We are, in fact, bombarded from many sides by idealized conceptions of how wonderful and all-encompassing love is, or *ought to be*:

- *Our Western conception of love* can be traced back to medieval codes of courtly behavior and chivalry that emphasized the profound importance of pinning one's affection solely upon one other idealized person, who is exalted to the point of appearing nearly superhuman. As recently as the late fifteenth century, royal and aristocratic young European men entered tournaments to win the "favor" of women whom they nominated as their amorous ideals—women who were actually unavailable because they were married or affianced to others! It was all a rather curious and courtly pantomime of manners. Yet social historians such as Denis de Rougemont point out that a great deal of our conceptualization of love comes down directly from the lyrics of love songs that were sung at the time. Whatever the underlying reasons, it is certain that the idealization of "falling in love" has become deeply ingrained in our culture. Today's song lyrics still tell us that our ideal life partner is waiting for us in the wings. When we find that person, our lives will be transformed permanently. "You're All I Need to Get By," one song tells us. "Love Will Keep Us Together" is another. Doubtless it is possible to be swept away by the power of falling in love, but that experience is not enough to sustain a long-term relationship.

- *Popular books and movies* also drive home an unrealistic belief in the power of love, once it is discovered, to overcome all life obstacles. Even modern romantic comedies like *Notting Hill* and *The Wedding Planner* (and many more you could name too) culminate in a final grand moment when two partners finally find each other, fall into each other's arms, and enter into a new life in which all romantic conflicts suddenly vanish. Love—preferably "love at first sight"—appears to be a resolution to all of life's problems— and that magical love power resides in some magical curative power that resides in our partners.

- *Our socially sanctioned rituals of mating and marriage* reinforce an unrealistically romantic concept of how ideal a monogamous relationship will be. Unless we keep our wits about us as we marry, we run the risk of believing for a time that one partner is capable of providing all the love we could ever want, and just about everything else we could ever need too. We know one young couple (and they are not unusual) who simply got swept away by the power of these rituals. In the euphoric days after they graduated from college, they announced their engagement. Their parents immediately put a vast machine into motion, starting with an engagement party and culminating in an elaborate, expensive wedding. A year later, they divorced. They had never actually wanted to get married *that* badly; they simply got swept along in a socially sanctioned romance-machine.

This idealization of love can land us in deep, guilt-infested waters where our loving relationships are at issue. We might be engaged in what is supposed to be a wonderful, self-sufficient monogamous relationship, yet find it deeply troubling to admit to ourselves that our partner does not fulfill all our emotional, erotic, or amatory needs.

In the end, many of us find it troubling that we are unable to suppress all our erotic desires for people outside our primary relationships. Try as we might, the erotic impulses that affected us in our earlier years reemerge, sometimes with the power to destabilize our relationships. Few of us can chase them away.

DURABLE, DURABLE EROS

For most of us (arguably, *all* of us) the erotic impulse does not automatically and placidly shut down the moment we marry or enter into a committed relationship. In varying degrees, most of us continue to feel attracted to people outside our primary relationships. This need to continue to feel erotically viable outside the relationship can express itself in a variety of ways. Some are socially sanctioned, others are not:

■ *Looking sexy and flirting.* Many men and women continue to enjoy expressing their erotic sides by continuing to dress in sexually alluring ways, even when married or in committed and monogamous relationships. Even though they might never "stray" from their relationships, they enjoy the sensation that they are still sexually attractive. Some people also retain the accoutrements that they used in their single days to attract partners: the expensive cars and jewelry, etc. Still other people like to flirt with people outside their primary relationships—perhaps in innocent ways, perhaps not. In many cases, a Darwinian game may be at work in these patterns. After all, when you or I take pains to appear attractive to people outside our monogamous relationships, we are showing our partners that we are still sexually viable entities. They had better pay attention and appreciate what they have in us, or someone else will!

■ *Enjoying the erotic input our culture provides.* In years past, women and men needed to go looking for "saucy" books, *Playboy, Playgirl,* or even *National Geographic* to find the fodder they needed to fuel their erotic fantasies. Today, we are surrounded by ways to enjoy erotic fantasies without actually engaging in infidelities. Movies, even those with milder ratings attached, present erotic content that would have been considered extreme only a decade ago. Our children have access to music videos that are bluer than that of any "blue" film of earlier years. If we turn on afternoon television, soap operas provide ready-made fantasies depicting very attractive men and women involved in complex mating rituals. Our erotic imaginations can fit right in and join the fray. And what about the Internet? It teems with erotic content that ranges from chat rooms to "hard" and "soft" pornography of all kinds.

- ■ *Carrying over mating and social rituals from the days before our committed relationships—even when doing so may place us in "harm's way."* One married woman we know dresses up and goes out with her "girlfriends" once a month to a bar, where they act they same way they did when they were single, though stopping short of actually pairing up with men. Similarly, many men get together with "buddies" to reenact activities from their singles days: attending boisterous bachelor parties, sporting events, or lunch at Hooters. Social sanctioning deems some of these activities as "harmless," but we do know that people who stretch such limits (often while consuming alcohol or other judgment-impairing substances) can be inviting infidelity and the complications it brings.

GUILT SURROUNDING OUR NEED FOR FRIENDSHIP

Similarly, many of us experience conflicts in our relationships when we realize that our sole partner cannot satisfy every interpersonal need in our lives. Even in monogamous relationships, we still need the presence of friends outside the relationship, often in some very specific ways. We know one woman who is married to a man who finds it difficult to become fully involved in the care of their young children, for example. To compensate, she has come to rely upon the friendship of a woman friend who is empathetic in this area. We also know a man who likes to play tennis—a sport his wife does not enjoy—so he has sought out the company of friends who share that interest to the exclusion of spending adequate time at home.

When our extramarital or extrarelational friends can be perceived as competitors for our affections, considerable conflict can arise, and tact is required if such friendships are to endure:

- Mark, who is married, maintains several close friendships with two women outside his marriage. One is a friend from college years—a woman who is a married mother. Another is a former work colleague—a woman who is in her sixties. "It would be difficult for me to have a friendship with a woman who might be seen as available and interested in something more than friendship with me," Mark tells us. "It would actually be impossible for me to start a friendship with a very attractive woman. My wife would go ballistic."

- Maryanne, a married woman, has gotten to be a regular lunch partner of Christopher, the director of the church choir in which she sings. Her husband is not troubled because Maryanne has told him that Christopher is gay. "Actually, I am not *certain* he is gay," Maryanne confided in us. By intimating to her husband that Christopher is homosexual, she has set up a context for her friendship that her husband will accept.

The least damaging way to enjoy such extramarital friendships is not to engage in concealments and subterfuges, but to talk openly with our primary partners about our friendships and even to bring our friends into social settings with our primary partners. When we engage in one-on-one socializing with such friends, it is often wise to share all the details of those times with our primary partners: explaining where we went, what we discussed, and so on. Fighting any tendency to conceal such friendships can go a long way toward preventing our partners from entering into unwarranted jealousy.

Overcoming the Fear That Accompanies Admission

Due to the social expectations and sanctions placed upon our primary love relationships, it becomes more understandable why many of us conceal our attraction for people on the outside.

Many of us begin to experience a kind of inner fear narrative, a series of "what if" suppositions based on fears of what might happen if we suddenly began to tell our partners that we are experiencing desires and emotions that are off-limits. We become afraid of dire outcomes that might result if we let our partners know about any "off-limits" thoughts and desires:

- We might be shown up to be less moral, less dependable, and less desirable than we were making ourselves out to be.

- Irreparable rifts will occur in our relationship. Our relationship might terminate right there on the spot.

- We might learn that our partners are dissatisfied with us too—that we are also not meeting *their* needs. Perhaps they too have needs that *we* are not meeting. That could be a real blow to our egos.

- We might encounter an unexpected, possibly uncontrollable reaction from our partners.

One approach to dealing with such fears is to remain "safely" hidden and never talk about the issues that are on our mind. ("If I don't mention what is on my mind, maybe we can just keep things the way they are indefinitely.")

TIME BOMBS AND ELEPHANTS

The problem is that when we bottle up problems in such ways instead of airing them, we usually create one of these two problems:

- A *"time bomb."* The problem we are avoiding does not go away. Instead, it becomes a ticking presence that is almost certain to explode someday, usually causing drastic harm to us and our relationship.

- An *"elephant in the living room."* This is a humorous term for something huge that is present in our lives that never gets mentioned. Perhaps you have a genuine drinking problem that you and your spouse simply never talk about. Perhaps you and your partner have not made love in years, but you don't ever talk about that. An elephant in the living room is a huge problem that you and your partner are aware of, but which never gets discussed.

The presence of such unspoken problems in a relationship is a strong predictor of its eventual demise. Serious problems and issues, if ignored, almost inevitably surface again to do greater damage than they could have if dealt with earlier.

CREATING A "CULTURE OF COMPLAINT"

Through years of innovative research, the marital therapist and researcher Dr. John Gottman has amassed copious data about what makes marriages succeed or fail. Today, he writes and lectures on the desirability of creating a "culture of complaint" in our love relationships. He has observed that when couples feel free to complain openly, airing their grievances to their partners, their relationship is actually *more* likely to endure than are relationships where problems are left unvoiced.

On the surface, the concept sounds negative. Isn't complaining a bad thing? What positive outcomes, after all, could result from bellyaching? After all, we are all taught over the years that it is bad, and destructive, to gripe or talk too much about our needs.

Dr. Gottman, however, is recommending something rather different: a climate in which both partners can air complaints without assigning blame or negatively criticizing the other person. Instead of repressing and bottling up dissatisfaction, they look openly at it. The idea is to create an atmosphere in which both partners feel free to say, "I have a problem. Do *we* have a problem?"

That question can be very important to any relationship. And its value increases many times over when we can ask it in an atmosphere that is free from guilt.

If that culture of complaint does not exist, airing any of our hidden problems or desires can be especially difficult. But if we can bring ourselves to open up these hidden areas for discussion, progress will almost always follow in our relationships.

Consider these case studies too, which give us insight into the power of bringing concealed problems into the light of day:

■ Jeannie had a strong need for physical comfort and intimacy that was not being met in her marriage to Jerry. She hesitated to bring the problem into the open for fear that she would be "clinging," "whining," or engaging in behavior she had dismissed as overly passive and "feminine." Yet she also realized that unless she talked over her issue with Jerry, her level of marital satisfaction would certainly decline and she might even be tempted to seek intimacy outside the relationship. When she initiated a discussion with Jerry about the issue, she learned that he also felt that intimacy was lacking in their life together. Through communication, they began to heal their relationship and move ahead on a new footing.

■ Martin, a man who was small and frail in his childhood years, continued to suffer from problems of low self-esteem as an adult, feeling himself to be unattractive. When he started a love partnership with a robust and very attractive man named Steve, he felt all the more insecure. When he and Steve went to parties where there were many other people, he felt jealous and extremely insecure in comparison to the other men there, fearing that Steve would almost surely find them more attractive than he. Over time, Martin continued to "bottle up" his feelings in this area, fearing that if he mentioned his insecurities, Steve would begin to find him less and less attractive. In time, feelings of estrangement began to intrude into the relationship—emotions that were probably attributable to Martin's inability to share his acute concerns and fears. Yet as was the case with Jeannie, mentioned above, he finally had the courage to open up his concerns, insecurities, and fears. As a result, his partnership with Steve stabilized, became durable, and now has lasted over a period of many years.

■ Claudia generally enjoyed the ease of her relationship with her attentive boyfriend, Frank, but she confided in friends that she found him to be somewhat "boring." In fact, she felt an intense need for sexual variety outside the relationship. She finally opened up and told him about it, even though she was certain he would be very deeply hurt and quite angry. The result was a quick dissolution of the relationship. (After all, the fairy-tale scenario of "living happily ever after" is not the best outcome to all intimate relationships.) A year after the relationship dissolved, both partners admitted that Claudia's truthfulness was a healthy thing that saved both of them from setting up false illusions of what their relationship was or might become. Their frank conversation was a difficult episode for them, but ultimately it helped them better understand what they needed and expected from intimate relationships.

It can take tremendous courage to bring your communication with your partner to this higher level. In Claudia's case, it required to her to admit feelings about herself that she did find admirable or desirable: a simple desire to experience more sexual variety with more exciting partners before settling into a long-term monogamous relationship.

FORGIVENESS

Forgiveness is the goal of confronting guilt, admitting our wrongdoing, creating a "culture of complaint," and following the other advice in this chapter. Yet forgiveness, we know, is a rather confusing concept:

■ After her husband admitted to having had an affair, Jennifer smiled and said, "I forgive you." She thought that was the case, but later learned otherwise when her anger resurfaced with new vehemence.

■ "Why can't you forgive me?" Sandy kept asking her lover after she had flirted openly with someone else at a party. In her mind, getting her lover to say the words "I forgive you" was the Band-Aid she was seeking—an immediate cure that would lay the problem to rest.

The fact is, "forgiveness" is not something that can be accomplished with just a few words, a handshake, or an agreement. Foregiveness is really something of a moving target: something that is more of a process than a quick cure.

For this reason, we would urge you to replace the idea of forgiveness with the concept of a "climate for forgiveness" in your loving relationship. You and your partner are evolving, imperfect people, after all. You do things that create tension for your partner, and the opposite is also true. You need to be seeking to understand and forgive at all times—gently and receptively, but without relinquishing your own values, expectations, and needs.

The goal should be to go on growing, through the active and warm process of forgiveness, to keep your relationship warm, evolving, and sound.

CHAPTER 13

HEALING AFTER AN INFIDELITY HAS TAKEN PLACE

Cassio's a proper man: let me see now:
To get his place and to plume up my will
In double knavery—How, how? Let's see:—
After some time, to abuse Othello's ear
That he is too familiar with his wife.
He hath a person and a smooth dispose
To be suspected, framed to make women false.
The Moor is of a free and open nature,
That thinks men honest that but seem to be so,
And will as tenderly be led by the nose
As asses are.
I have't. It is engender'd. Hell and night
Must bring this monstrous birth to the world's light.

> —Iago, plotting Othello's demise, in *Othello*,
> Act I, Scene 3

EARLIER CHAPTERS OF THIS book have focused on the psychology of the Othello response as it pertains to unfounded jealousy: one partner becomes jealous, perhaps obsessively or violently so, despite the fact that his or her partner has not "strayed" or engaged in an infidelity with someone else.

We will change that focus in this chapter to ask what might be some very pressing question in many people's lives:

- What can you do to mend and recover if infidelity has actually taken place?

- How can you determine whether recovery is even possible?

- How can you reverse the Othello response?

- How can your make your relationship healthy again?

ASK THE BIG QUESTION FIRST

If you or your partner have engaged in an actual infidelity outside of your primary love relationship, you both have some very difficult work to do, and some difficult times ahead.

The first, overriding question is whether you and your partner have the commitment and desire to preserve your relationship. At times, both partners will understand very early on after an infidelity that they will either try, or *not* try, to preserve the relationship that was violated, as these case studies show:

A TWO-FAMILY MAN

We recently heard a rather remarkable story of a seventy-year-old man who had, for years, maintained two households. One was with his wife and their children. A second household included another woman, with whom he also had a family. Apparently this man was largely guiltless about living in two places, in a very complicated way. Most remarkable of all was the fact that his wife actually agreed to live in the arrangement. Apparently she felt so guilty that her husband had "strayed" that she went on for years trying to "win him back" and putting up with the arrangement.

- A man named Sam tells us that he knew and accepted the reality that going to bed with Karen was an irrevocable step that would quickly end his very troubled marriage with Portia. Once he had done it, there would be no healing his marriage or turning back. It was a point of no return for him.

- Charlotte and her husband had been experiencing marital difficulties for more than a year, but had remained faithful to each other. Then while on a business trip, Charlotte had a one-night stand with a man she met. But the experience had the effect of reorienting her toward her marriage. She returned home to her husband and family with a great sense of determination to mend her marriage and "save" it.

Many other scenarios are possible after an infidelity has occurred. Some of them can be quite complex and not easily resolved:

- When Mary came home from work early one day, she found her husband Roger in bed with one of her best friends. She immediately said she wanted a divorce, but Roger was more conciliatory, saying he saw no reason why the marriage could not be salvaged. Mary didn't see how.

- Scott came home to dinner one evening and told his wife Pamela that he had fallen in love with another woman and was moving out that night, leaving her and the children. Pamela was convinced that Scott was "going through a phase," that he was having his midlife crisis and that he would self-correct and return home in a week or two if she could only be patient.

FORGIVENESS

Forgiveness can be defined in many ways. It can be defined as:

- To make a clean slate of a debt.

- To let go of any grievance or retaliatory impulse that results from injury or injustice.

In the context of a love relationship, to forgive means to create a renewed sense of balance and goodwill in the relationship. Where the Othello response has been an issue, forgiveness can also mean letting go of any grudges we are carrying over from the past and any incipient revenge fantasies to "right" past wrongs.

Overall, the first step toward forgiveness is to forgive yourself. Try to let go of self-blame and guilt about things that were done and things that were left undone. This can clear the slate toward starting the difficult process of forgiving your partner, if forgiving needs to take place.

PUTTING THINGS BACK TOGETHER

Whatever our initial intentions after an infidelity has taken place, a variety of different realities can intrude, altering our view of how things are supposed to go in the recovery process. Chief among these is the presence of children. Even when colliding parents feel they are free to simply split up and end a relationship, in most cases they are not truly able to do so if kids are in the picture. Even if a divorce occurs, the relationship will still be there—in a drastically changed way, but certainly not gone entirely. (Granted, one parent could disappear and never be heard from again, but that is a scenario that occurs more often on soap operas than in real life.) Then there are the stages of recovery, which seem like slippery ground for the couple trying to pass through them:

- One day one partner is determined to preserve the relationship, the next day is angry and convinced it is not worth a try.

- One day trust seems to be returning to the relationship. The next day it is replaced by enmity.

- One day both partners feel happy to be at work and going about their daily routines. But when they return home at night, the presence of their problem suddenly overwhelms them.

- Sexual intimacy returns for a time, then vanishes into a haze of distrust and deepened feelings of betrayal.

This is a horrible period for any couple to get through, but a necessary one. Any infidelity ushers in a period of extreme uncertainty and instability. If the relationship or marriage is to endure, a climate of forgiveness needs to be established and trust gradually regained. It is a process that demands a great deal of time. There are complex issues to be identified and resolved: issues of trust, guilt, fear, anger, and more.

As we noted in the previous chapter, the partners who have been "wronged" sometimes attempt to duck out of this exhausting process, saying to a partner, "Okay, you had sex (or an affair) with someone else. I forgive you. Let's just forget it and just move on." In nearly all such cases, easy attempts at avoidance only create more "time bombs" that later explode. For a time, both partners may manage to deny that they are facing a huge problem that needs to be addressed, not ignored. They might be able to pretend to be looking the other way, but the problem is growing more potent and more likely to trigger future disruptions, including further infidelities on the part of either partner, or even a sudden dissolution of the relationship:

- Often, the partner who "forgives" has an increased tendency to engage in a future retaliatory affair. Sometimes the underlying goal is to issue a covert warning: "You did it, but didn't you realize that *I* can do it too?"

- At other times, the straying partner who was "forgiven" never passes through the period of introspection that is required to understand why he or she entered into infidelity. Because the hard work of self-analysis has not been done, there is a greater likelihood that the problematic behavior will recur.

If simple, one-shot forgiveness will not work, what kind of process is needed before healing can occur—if healing is possible at all? The uncomfortable truth is that a very intense process of sharing needs to be embarked upon if the relationship is to be saved:

- The partner who "strayed" and engaged in the infidelity needs to be ready to reveal and discuss—in detail—exactly what took place between him or herself and the person(s) with whom infidelity occurred.

- The person who did not "stray" needs to hear everything about what took place, even if he or she believes that it would be less painful to leave it all unexplored and unspoken. Very often, the betrayed person is intensely curious about what truly happened and almost desperately needs to know.

This kind of intense sharing and back-and-forth discussion

cannot be accomplished in just one sitting or one afternoon. It needs to go on for quite a long time if trust is ever to be won back. Both parties need to go through an intense process of trust-mending.

The process cannot be termed *complete* disclosure, but rather *constant* disclosure. The person who has been "wronged" needs to know just what happened, where it happened, how it happened, and, if possible, *why* it happened too. From the other side of the equation, the person who "did wrong" needs to go through the exhausting process of explaining all those things and actively seeking forgiveness.

> ### "YOU ARE AS SICK AS YOUR SECRETS"
>
> This expression is a way of reminding AA members that bringing their drinking problem out into the open is the only way to loosen its power over their lives. And we do know that secrets tend to become more powerful over time. If we bottle them up, they often begin to exert greater and greater control over us. The same holds true with our unspoken desires—if we can courageously discuss them with our partners instead of bottling them up, their power to do us harm is diminished.

At times, this process seems almost punitive. The "wronged" partner sometimes needs to ask the same question again and again while the delinquent partner becomes impatient and says, "What, that again? I already told you all about that. Let's move on!"

Regaining trust is a major life process, not unlike recovering from the death of a loved one or learning that you have a life-threatening disease. Like those processes, it does not often move forward in a neat, linear way. One day your anger subsides and you think you have turned a corner toward recovery; then the next day, you are furious all over again. One day you feel you are ready to forgive a partner who wronged you; and the next day, you are irate again and conclude that forgiveness is impossible.

With time and a great deal of patience and goodwill, emotions of intense blame or intense guilt may subside. A collaborative atmosphere may finally develop around the issue, a *forgiving climate*. To get there, it is necessary to keep admitting and explaining wrongs, owning up to our faults, seeking forgiveness, and striving to replenish the goodwill that has been drained from the relationship.

In this process, you and your partner are continually trying to exercise forgiveness and exorcise blame from your lives together by continually doing the hard work of trying to understand what went wrong.

"I AM NOT WHAT I AM"

I will wear my heart upon my sleeve
For daws to peck at: I am not what I am."
—Iago

By any measure, these are extraordinary words. On the surface, they seem to warn us that Iago will not be what he seems to be to those around him. He will never show his real self. He will be all smoke, distortion, and deception.

Yet we need to remember that Iago did not say, "I will not seem to be what I am." He actually tells us that he will not *be* who he is.

And there are no clearer depictions of what it means to enter into the dark world of the Othello response, where you are not what you are, you do not do what you do, do not love the person you love.

Rather than acting reasonably by learning the truth or trusting his wife, this is the path that Othello chooses to pursue. He chooses to be something horrible, alien, dangerous, and ultimately fatal to his faithful wife and his world.

A CASE STUDY: CLEO AND LEE

It is now more than six months since Lee confessed to his wife Cleo that he had been having an affair with another woman — an affair that he had decided to end. Lee characterized the affair as "casual and only physical," meaning that he had no interest in maintaining an enduring relationship with this other woman. He saw the affair as something that "just happened." However, there had been a lot of lying and concealment in the way he had conducted the affair. On one occasion, he had told Cleo that he was going on a business trip to Atlanta, but had actually gone to a beach resort in Florida with this "other woman." It was a lie that had required him to engage in some complex subterfuge to conceal where he was staying, where he could be contacted, and so on.

Lee, with good reason, was quite worried that he might have done irreparable damage to his marriage. Still, he ended the affair and told Cleo what had happened, a step that required considerable conflict on his part. For a time, he had seriously been thinking of concealing his affair from his wife. When Lee told Cleo about his affair and explained that it was now over and that he was seeking forgiveness, Cleo was devastated and extremely angry. Lee, from his end, had miscalculated the intensity of the reaction he would get from her, somehow believing that if he confessed about the affair and said it was over and he was "turning over a new leaf," he could somehow be forgiven quickly. He and his wife, he thought, would quickly get on with their lives once the air was cleared.

Yet six months after Lee's confession, the recovery process was still quite intense. Cleo continued to ask Lee many questions about his affair. On the night Lee started his affair with this other woman, where did they have sex? Did the woman make the first sexual overture, or did Lee? How many times did they have sex? How did they have sex? What was it like to have sex with this other woman? What kind of contraception did they use? Was there a chance that Lee had contracted HIV or a sexually transmitted disease with this other woman and given it to Cleo? Had Lee kept and hidden any pictures of this other woman or any letters from her? Did he ever hear from her? Was she an intelligent woman? What were the chances that Cleo and Lee would run into her, and what would Lee do if they did?

Sometimes Cleo's questions became repetitive, which irritated Lee. Sometimes the questions were angry ("Why are you such a jerk?"), but Lee needs to suffer those questions too. At other times the questions that recur are harrowingly honest and direct ("Why did you do this to me?").

The process moved forward, then slipped backward again. It was weeks into the process before Lee explained that he had taken the other woman to Florida and lied to Cleo about where he was at the time. That revelation proved to be a great setback with a real potential to end their marriage. Such lies about past events are truly devastating to their victims once they are revealed, making the sufferer think, "My past and the events that I believed took place did not take place. What other falsehoods are still waiting to be uncovered? How can I trust you now?"

Yet over time, the trust appeared to be mending to some degree. It appeared likely that the relationship would be preserved and go on. It will be a very long time before complete trust is reestablished. Can absolute healing ever be achieved? Possibly, possibly not. One positive sign is that Lee and Cleo are engaging in an active process of forgiveness. Without this difficult routine, there is no hope at all of preserving the relationship.

Such dire events change relationships forever. Even if we heal, there is never any chance of pretending that the rift that occurred never happened. It will forever remain a chapter in the relationship or marriage, a phase that cannot—and should not—be forgotten or ignored.

Often, mending processes like the one that Lee and Cleo are going through can be helped by the assistance and intervention of a mediator or marital therapist, someone who can provide impartial guidance and a neutral forum where both partners can air their fears, concerns, anger, and frustration. The presence of an experienced outsider cannot dispel all the pain and discomfort from the hard work that needs to be done, yet might be able to expedite the process and provide feedback on how well the healing process is moving ahead.

THE DANGER OF SIMPLY CALLING IT QUITS

As already noted, failing to engage fully in the difficult process of healing creates a ticking time bomb that can cause severe damage later on. There is still another troubling reality to confront about the healing process. It is the fact that if we simply call it quits and walk away from a troubled relationship without attempting to understand what went wrong, we often open ourselves up to a range of similar problems in our new relationships.

It is tempting to simply think, "That person was an abusive jerk; I'm glad it is over," and then consider that the problem is in the past. Yet where something as traumatic as an infidelity took place, some personal analysis and active self-healing are in order. We need to think about what went wrong and strive to understand the lessons of the experience.

Otherwise, we are much more likely to experience disruptions in future relationships:

■ If you have been betrayed and just charge on into other relationships, you might come to believe that there is something "wrong" with you. Future lovers will probably cheat on you too.

■ You might come to believe unreliable sexual stereotypes, believing that "all men" or "all women" are promiscuous, unreliable, and prone to cheat on their lovers.

■ In an ongoing effort to go on processing the problems that arose in the troubled relationship you left, you might form a new partnership with someone who will behave in the same way as the partner you just left behind. After leaving an unreliable and alcoholic man, for example, you might immediately forge a new relationship with another unreliable or substance-abusing man. Or after leaving a relationship with a very beautiful woman who cheated on you, you might tend to start a relationship with a new woman who is also very beautiful, just to establish that you are capable of sustaining the interest of someone who is very much sought after by other males. Such patterns can do considerable harm to you and also to new relationships with partners who are becoming drawn into the problems that remain unresolved from your previous relationships.

■ You might simply become reluctant to commit again to a loving relationship. When you have been betrayed, it is easy to say that it hurt so much, why would you ever open yourself to that kind of damage again? This is a catastrophic course of action to take in life—to cut yourself off from love and intimacy because of unhappiness suffered in the past.

■ You might experience another eruption of the Othello response. If you have been betrayed in a relationship, you might bring to future relationships a drive to be overly vigilant, protective, or jealous of your new love interests. Is that understandable? Of course it is. Yet seen from the perspective of those who will love you in the future, you are carrying with you a considerable burden and liability that has a very real potential to harm them in the years ahead.

So we see that the "hard work" of processing the lessons of infidelities is necessary even if a relationship ends.

COMPASSION

People who have just been betrayed by their partners usually enter into a "flooding" state in which they can only dwell on the enormity of what has taken place. They no longer remember the good things that occurred in the relationship in the past.

Hard as it can be to muster at such times, compassion offers a good place to begin the recovery process. With compassion, you try to see your partner fully. If he or she has been unfaithful, can you identify what is behind that problem? Is it something in their specific history, in their family, in their character? What's this person looking for?

Despite what has been done to you, can you strive to understand and have compassion for that person? Can you understand their weakness, their loneliness?

Secondly (and this is an even harder assignment), can you identify what your role was in causing the problem? What did you do to usher in the problem, to cause it to occur? Could you have seen it coming? Did you have blinders on? Were you in denial about problems that existed?

It is easy to assign blame to the other person, far harder to consider how you contributed to the problem. Such questions may help you exercise compassion, both toward your partner and yourself. In a compassionate climate, healing can start.

The Dawning of a New Day

If the relationship can be preserved, a new day can finally dawn when trust has been regained and things become stable again. However, there are some realities that need to be understood within the context of any relationship that has been rocked by infidelity. Let's take a closer look:

- *Things will not get back to the way they used to be.* This is one myth of forgiveness: the notion that a couple can work things through and restore the relationship to "where it used to be." That is a false expectation. Once an infidelity has taken place, you and your partner are in a new place that requires new rules, new attitudes, and new expectations.

- *Both partners need to develop new habits and routines to support each other and foster trust.* For obvious reasons, issues of trust and autonomy come to the forefront after an infidelity has taken place. If a partner "strayed" while on a business trip, for example, both partners would do well to discuss and implement a series of routines the next time a business trip occurs. They might schedule regular phone-in times, e-mails, and other routines so that the partner at home continues to feel the partner's commitment and concern, even though he or she is in the same context where an infidelity took place.

- *The topic of the infidelity cannot become "off-limits" or "out of bounds."* Both partners would do well to make an open agreement that the issue can be brought up at any time, despite the fact that doing so might be uncomfortable.

Recovery is an ongoing process with no end date. When we go through the hard period of healing and forgiving, we internally long for a final day, the day when we can finally say, "That difficult process is now over. We are okay now." Unfortunately, that is another false goal. A relationship that has been tested in the fire of unfaithfulness must maintain a "subprocess" of ongoing recovery, even when things appear sound and stable again.

In time, your relationship will arrive in a new place, one as secure and stable as the one you occupied before problems struck. It might even be *more* secure. Often, the hard work of mending and putting together required you and your partner to confront and work through difficult issues that needed to be dealt with anyway: issues of expectations, sexual intimacy, and trust, to name just a few. But the infidelity will not disappear. It is a chapter you went through in your relationship—a troubling one, to be sure—that must take its place alongside all the other experiences that make up the history of any enduring relationship.

A THOUGHTFUL DEFINITION OF MARRIAGE

Marriage is an unfolding, dynamic loving state comprised of two human beings who are full of desires and emotion and each with a unique history and set of beliefs. A marriage needs frequent renewal and support. It needs to be redesigned, renegotiated, and recreated. Marriage grows stronger as familiarity, fondness, and mutual attention grow. Marriage grows stronger as each person takes greater responsibility, admits faults, forgives, and helps to solve problems.

PART FIVE
DEEPENING OUR UNDERSTANDING

Preventing and healing the Othello response hinges on communication, healing, and the other skills we have explored in the earlier chapters of this book.

Our ability to prevent and manage the Othello response improves when we go beyond such practical considerations and ask some deeper questions too:

- Can we arrive at a deeper level of understanding of human jealousy and the role it plays in our lives?

- Where does jealousy come from?

- Can it help us as well as do us harm?

- Does it contain lessons that can help us live and love more fully?

In the chapters that follow, we will explore the findings of evolutionary psychologists on these questions. We will then consider ancient teachings about living well, drawing on sources such as Aristotle and Saint Thomas Aquinas.

CHAPTER 14
THE GOOD AND BAD
FACES OF JEALOUSY

Let it be borne in mind how infinitely complex and close-fitting are the mutual relations of all organic beings to each other and to their physical conditions of life. Can it, then, be thought improbable, seeing that variations useful to man have undoubtedly occurred, that other variations useful in some way to each being in the great and complex battle of life, should sometimes occur in the course of thousands of generations? If such do occur, can we doubt (remembering that many more individuals are born than can possibly survive) that individuals having any advantage, however slight, over others, would have the best chance of surviving and of procreating their kind? On the other hand, we may feel sure that any variation in the least degree injurious would be rigidly destroyed. This preservation of favourable variations and the rejection of injurious variations, I call Natural Selection.

—From chapter four, "Natural Selection," *The Origin of the Species by Natural Selection: Or, The Preservation of Favored Races in the Struggle for Life* by Charles Darwin, 1859

WHEN WE READ THIS passage from Charles Darwin's *Origin of the Species*, we witness the articulation of an idea so cataclysmic, it will forever change the world. Suddenly, millions of seemingly unordered biological truths can be grouped into a new and cohesive context.

Everything we have become, everything we *are*, is the result of natural selection.

It is remarkable how widely accepted Darwin's fundamental truth has become in our world:

- Even lay people today understand that animals like the green leaf hopper acquired their color gradually over millennia. Over the course of tens of millions of years, nature has favored leaf hoppers that have a little more green pigmentation than other leaf hoppers. The less-green individuals, statistically speaking, were more likely to stand out visually from vegetation and were more likely to be eaten by predators. Through all of evolution, the statistical probability that slightly greener individuals would survive became significant to the point where all leaf hoppers are now bright green.

- We understand that the extraordinary plumage of male peacocks is not simply beautiful, but is another gift of natural selection. Somewhere in the dim past of peacock evolution, males who possessed flashier feathers than other males fared better in mating rituals. (To this day, they still do.) The more ostentatious males simply managed to mate with more females than the duller fellows, so over history bright plumage became a reinforced trait. Today, there are very few male peacocks incapable of putting on a startling, fireworkslike display of feather power.

When we rise each morning and look in the mirror at ourselves, we encounter a complex being who is not only the result of who our parents were, but of millions of selective events that took place over the course of human evolution, and possibly before. Our specific forebears were not the genetic "also-rans" whose lines perished when they proved incapable of securing and protecting mates or producing offspring. No, our ancestors were those who won at the procreative game and passed their genetic material down to us.

What enabled these successful earlier humans, whose genetic material we carry, to succeed at the mating game? Some of their traits are those we find positive, such as physical attractiveness, intelligence, and robust health. Other characteristics are not so pleasant to consider, such as aggressiveness, success in physical combat, and cunning. And then there is another unattractive trait that surely equipped our distinct progenitors to pass their genetic imprint down to us: jealousy.

CUCKOLDRY: WHEN MEN ARE BETRAYED

Nearly all societies, from Africa to Alaska, from Italy to Ireland, relegate a man whose lover has cheated on him to a lowered social status. In many cultures, such a man experiences trouble attracting a substitute wife or partner. If he wants to mate successfully again, he can choose from several options to restore his status so he can again attract another woman. He can move or otherwise conceal his history of having an unfaithful lover. Or he can exercise the option of taking violent action against his former partner and/or her new lover, because revenge offers him a way to regain his former status.

Then there are issues of paternity. When children are present as the result of infidelity, the stakes for the cuckolded man rise exponentially. The fear of having invested energy to preserve another man's progeny is too much to bear.

Women get "cuckolded" too. Their husbands father children with other women. Some women, like men, behave violently when that happens.

Just watch daytime TV and you'll see. Apparently, the greatest shame a man or woman can incur is being made to appear reproductively absurd.

Our forbears were jealous. Or at least jealous enough to achieve the following results in highly competitive human mating rituals:

- *Mating.* Both men and women drove away competitors and won sexual access to their partners.

- *Protection.* Men were able to keep male competitors at bay during both procreative and child-rearing years.

- *Sustenance.* Women drove other women away to long-running mating patterns with males who had proved capable of both fathering and providing protection and material support to the mothers of their offspring and to their offspring as well.

- *Promiscuity.* It has equipped not only men, but women too, to enjoy greater odds that their genetic material will be passed forward to ensuing generations. (Men, by mating with many partners; women, by having "backup" mates waiting to step in when their primary males are killed or die. Remember, we are talking about patterns that developed millennia ago.)

We may not be "slaves" to all the hereditary traits we carry around with us, or to all the genetic material we have inherited. Yet we may be much more indebted to our forebears and resemble them more closely than we realize. As genetic material is passed on from generation to generation, the numerical advantage enjoyed by people who are able to mate and procreate successfully can become quite staggering.

SEXUAL SELECTION

After describing the forces that shaped our physical evolution from our forebears, Charles Darwin next turned his mind to the issues of sexual selection. Let's consider this quote from one of his late works, *The Descent of Man*, published in 1871: "We are, however, here concerned only with sexual selection. This depends on the advantage which certain individuals have over others of the same sex and species solely in respect of reproduction. When . . . the two sexes differ in structure in relation to different habits of life, they have no doubt been modified through natural selection."

It is only twelve years after *The Origin of the Species*. Darwin continues to break new territory. He is telling us that in addition to the natural selection that allowed certain of our ancestors to avoid being eaten (and to adapt to extremes of temperature and to otherwise survive), natural selection was working on another level too. It was also determining whom among our progenitors were best equipped to win at the mating game.

Natural selection smiled upon certain individuals due to their physical traits, such as strength, reproductive viability, and even sense of smell and vision, which aided both males and females in locating mates. (Remember, we are talking about the pre-Internet age when no dating services were available on-line!)

Darwin was also beginning to suspect that certain outlooks, behaviors, and psychological traits had their role to play in mate selection as well:

- Certain mating rituals evolved that allowed our progenitors to effectively express sexual interest in one another, reject unsatisfactory partners, and then produce offspring with selected partners.

■ Patterns of aggression arose too, in which rival suitors claimed precedence over others in the competition for viable mating partners (males ever the more aggressive, much as we would like to say otherwise).

■ Social structures developed that supported the nurturing of offspring. For instance, some societies encompassed a social "safety net" that allowed young to be cared for by individuals who were not the parents, thereby increasing the reproductive capabilities of individuals in their prime breeding years.

At the time of his death in 1882, Charles Darwin was still unleashing great truths that remain controversial today. One Darwin obituary, written by Thomas Huxley in the scientific journal *Nature*, sums up his contributions to human thinking: "He found a great truth, trodden under foot, reviled by bigots, and ridiculed by all the world; he lived long enough to see it, chiefly by his own efforts, irrefragably established in science, inseparably incorporated with the common thoughts of men, and only hated and feared by those who would revile, but dare not."

DARWIN A CENTURY LATER

Predictably, Darwin's seismic thinking did not die with him. Over the century and a half since his death, it has influenced the research of geneticists, social anthropologists, physical anthropologists, sociologists, ethnologists, endocrinologists, and more.

For the purposes of this book, we need to turn our attention away from the researchers who have continued to study the physical evolution and adaptations of mankind. Their work, though certainly fascinating, lies to the side of the purpose of this book, which is to explore people's behavior, not physical adaptations.

We will instead explore the research and findings of scientists who have amplified Darwin's theories of sexual selection. We call these researchers *evolutionary psychologists*, a fascinating pairing of terms if ever there was one. Who are these evolutionary psychologists? They are scientists who:

- Explore the psychological makeup and behaviors of our successful ancestors who "won" the game of evolution and passed their genes on to us.

- Analyze the inherited behavioral patterns and psychological traits we might have inherited from these successful ancients.

FUNDAMENTAL BELIEFS OF EVOLUTIONARY PSYCHOLOGY

Do we know for certain that evolution has shaped our psychological and instinctive makeup, not merely our physical configurations? The answer is, we don't. Compelling as the logic may be behind the idea, it is really just a theory advanced by evolutionary psychologists.

Consider these five fundamental tenets of evolutionary psychology, developed by Professors Leda Cosmides and John Tooby, leading researchers in the field of evolutionary psychology at the University of California at Santa Barbara:

- *Principle 1. The brain is a physical system.* It functions as a computer. Its circuits are designed to generate behavior and motions that are appropriate to environmental circumstances.

- *Principle 2. Our neural circuits were designed by natural selection.* They evolved to solve problems that our ancestors faced during our species' evolutionary history.

- *Principle 3. Consciousness is just the tip of the iceberg.* Most of what goes on in our minds is hidden from us.

- *Principle 4. Different neural circuits are specialized.* They are configured for solving different adaptive problems.

- *Principle 5. Our modern skulls house a Stone Age mind.* Natural selection, the process that designed our brains, takes a long time to design a circuit of any complexity. A lot of the circuitry we still carry around is very old.*

Such evolutionary psychologists believe that today's evolved humans possess a certain number of brain circuits, developed through natural selection, that equip them to best pass their genetic material down to ensuing generations. What are these successful traits that may have become "hardwired" into our brains during the course of human evolution—the success traits that have made the difference between our sexually successful ancestors and the "also-runs" whose genetic material withered and dried up with their bones?

Let's take a closer look.

---

* Leda Cosmides and John Tooby, *Evolutionary Psychology: A Primer* (http://www.psych.ucsb.edu/research/cep/primer.html).

Robert Wright and *The Moral Animal*

Robert Wright, an editor at *The New Republic,* can be credited with placing this "New Darwinism" firmly in the popular consciousness with his book, *The Moral Animal: Why We Are the Way We Are: The New Science of Evolutionary Psychology.* It offers both a popularization of Darwin's theories for general readers and the first contemporary manual on evolutionary psychology. We might call it a user's handbook for understanding the hardwired sex circuits in the brain. Upon its publication in 1994, *The Moral Animal* made headlines and aroused controversy.

In black and white, Wright spelled out some troubling conclusions from the research conducted by evolutionary psychologists. Let's take a closer look at what he had to say.

What Men and Women Want

In *The Moral Animal,* Wright reports that the instinctual and psychological traits that have allowed men and women to reproduce most effectively (thereby passing their genetic material to the maximum number of individuals in succeeding generations and becoming evolutionary "winners") are in reality quite different.

The men who fared best at the game of evolution were:

- *Reproductively viable* enough to father as many children as possible.

- *Aggressive* enough to reach the apexes of their social orders and fight off competitors for female's sexual attention.

- *Wealthy* enough to provide support for their mates and offspring.

(Remember, "wealth" can mean many things in primitive society, such as an ample supply of food or land to cultivate.)

■ *Vigilant and violent* enough to keep competitors at bay.

■ *Attracted principally to young females* in their prime reproductive years, so their genetic material goes where it will produce the maximum number of descendants.

■ *Above all, promiscuous.* For men, genetic success hinged on the ability to mate with many partners.

Furthermore, evolutionary psychologists would like us to accept the idea that men still possess these traits. They are the factors that allowed our male forefathers to win out in the pachinko-like game of human evolution. They are part of contemporary men too.

The women who fared best at the game of evolution were:

■ *Reproductively viable* enough to bear as many offspring as possible. This means something different for women than it does for men, of course, because women can bear only one child (or three or four at most) at a time. Women who had a hard time becoming impregnated were less successful in the evolutionary sweepstakes.

■ *Attractive and youthful* enough to be sought after by males.

■ *Socially adept* enough to assure that their offspring would be well cared for. According to much research reported by Wright, reproductively successful women have been those

> 1) who found the protection of strong, well-resourced males and, 2) who, to a lesser extent, built coalitions with other women and backup care providers for their children.

Admittedly, these viewpoints are drawn from prehistory and add up to a view of relationships that is both paternalistic and sexist. We need to remind ourselves that, through history, there have been countless exceptions to such "rules." Many reproductively successful females (members of nineteenth-century royalty, for example) did not hang around their homes caring for their children; they had relatively little to do with their children after giving birth to them. History also tells us that many men have not been promiscuous, but loyal to just one woman, even after her childbearing years had passed.

There are always exceptions to rules, yet the fact remains that if we follow the laws of evolutionary psychology to their natural conclusions, some kind of dualist view is bound to arise regarding the roles men and women play in mating and love. At base, the dualism is due to the fact that women, unlike men, give birth to children from their own bodies, and they are capable of parenting far fewer children than are men, who could theoretically father thousands upon thousands of children.

IAGO'S BESTIAL LANGUAGE

When Iago sprang from Shakespeare's imagination, he appeared with a very peculiar, particular way of expressing himself. From the moment he walks upon the stage, his language is distasteful and repugnant.

Consider how he tells Brabantio in Act I, Scene 1, that Desdemona has eloped: "Even now, now, very now, an old black ram is topping your white ewe."

A moment later, the language Iago addresses at Brabantio becomes even more obscene: "I am one, sir, that comes to tell you your daughter and the Moor are now making the beast with two backs."

He speaks of rams, ewes, asses, cats, flies, dogs, monkeys, wolves, and other animals, often depicted taking part in, or victimized by, activities that are cruel or obscene. Iago's bestial language repeatedly causes us to recoil. We flinch from him, fascinated as we are by his power and influence over Othello. Yet we are also attracted to the horrible images he conjures up, just as we become attracted to our fantasies of our lovers engaged in sexual acts with other people. As much as we want to turn away, it is difficult. And once we have looked, horrid images continue to play in our minds as we are titillated and lured into his influence. We are trapped, just as we can become snared in the coils of the Othello response. In its horror lies part of its allure.

It could even be that by using all this talk of beasts, Shakespeare is showing us that when we follow Iago's path, we become beasts ourselves, turning away from all that can be good and noble in human hearts.

EVOLUTIONARY BACKLASH

Like any herald who tells us things we might rather not know, Wright aroused a lot of anger from many quarters. Many fundamentalist Christians objected to *The Moral Animal*'s reporting of studies that implied that patterns of human love evolved and were not given from God. Other critics accused Wright of being a woman-hater whose views fell in line with those other "social Darwinists" who were often racists too.

These are false accusations. Wright tells us awful things about women, but he tells us equally awful things about men too, on roughly an equal basis. We can believe his findings or we can reject them, but as his views are supported and/or refuted by further research, his views deserve dispassionate consideration and thought.

WHAT EMERGES FROM THE DUALISM OF EVOLUTIONARY PSYCHOLOGY

If we accept the notion that men and women have been "hardwired" differently, certain conclusions flow logically afterward. They are often not enjoyable to think about, but we need to take a hard look at them as we consider the roots of the Othello response.

It just might be that some Othello response traits are imprinted into our brains as clearly as the little patterns on microchips:

- *Jealousy.* Not nice to think about, is it? Yet if we accept post-Darwinian conclusions, it becomes clear that jealousy is a great predictor of genetic success. When women are jealous, they intimidate and scare other potential females away from their male partners. When men are jealous and pro-tective, they chase away rivals and assure that more of their genetic material is passed down. Our genes are like aggres-sive little egos, ever striving to move ahead, outlive us, and move ever onward through time.

- *Ageism in men.* As noted above, males gravitate toward younger females, or at least toward females who are in their prime reproductive years. That's sexist, not nice to think about. But there is a genetic explanation for this kind of behavior.

- *Ageism in women.* Ageism is more complex where women are concerned. At first blush, it might be tempting to say that the age of a man would not matter to a woman, as long as he remains reproductively viable and, in the case of our ancestors, strong enough to protect her and her offspring and provide sustenance. Yet there is evidence to suggest that females (both human females and lower primates too) are often attracted to established, older males. This is true in chimpanzee societies, where an older male occupies the

EVOLUTIONARY PSYCHOLOGY IN SONG

"I Love, I Love, I Love My Wife, But Oh You Kid!"

—One of the most popular songs of the year 1904. Music by Harry von Tilzer, lyrics by Jimmy Lucas

alpha position and enjoys free sexual access to the females. There are similarities to human societies as well, where older, secure males are still viewed as viable sexual partners for younger females.

■ *Fickleness*. Many studies have confirmed that male animals consistently prefer to mate with new females of their species. When offered a choice of cows to mate with, for example, bulls always opt for new partners over old. This kind of selectiveness (picking the new, discarding the old) appears not to be as strong a factor in female animals. It might be called a *male* trait.

■ *Ganging up and politicking*. Males and females alike form coalitions to keep would-be mates away from their partners. We see this again in chimpanzee societies, where a dominant male may select a "deputy" to help drive away or kill other males who are seeking sexual access to females. This "deputy" might be allowed some sexual rights in exchange. Females can behave similarly, ganging up on younger females who appear attractive to their mates. Yet evolutionary psychologists document that violent outcomes, including physical attacks, are more likely to arise from coalitions formed by males.

■ *Aggression and intimidation*. Both men and women scare

away rivals and assure sexual access to either their current mates or their intended ones. Social structures surrounding mating provide a clear indication of this. Male sports, in particular, have always provided a forum for men to demonstrate their aggressive and intimidating potential over other men, traits that establish their high place in the sexual "pecking order" and may qualify them to compete for the most attractive women off the field. In contrast, females tend to intimidate other females by flaunting their beauty, sexual viability, and attractiveness.

HOW MEN KEEP RIVALS AWAY

When a competitor arrives and makes a play for a man's female partner, outright aggression sometimes does the job of driving him away. When that doesn't work, the threatened male usually begins to tell half-truths to denigrate the competitor's worth. Most often, the male who is challenged will tell his mate that this other man is:

- Poor and without resources

- Lacking in ambition

- Driving a cheap car

Interesting: Women hardly ever engage in similar behavior to color their partner's impression of other women and if they do, it rarely works.

Source: 1990 study conducted by evolutionary psychologist David M. Buss

We can see further evidence of these unhappy truths in movies and popular culture, which portray the passive, nonaggressive male or female "nerds" as reproductive also-runs who rarely can secure a sexual partner. Male nerds are not aggressive; female nerds are not comely enough to attract men. If and when these second-class people manage to mate, their success if usually presented in comic, laugh-inducing ways.

■ *Deception.* Men have been reproductively rewarded for lots of deceitful activities, including exaggerating their physical strength and health, making false statements regarding what they do to earn their livelihoods, lying or implying that they have had many previous sex partners to document their sexual capabilities to potential mates, and engaging in exaggerated displays of wealth. Women, in their turn, have lied about their age. They have pretended to be less smart than they are (with the unstated belief that if they appear to be dumb, men will believe it will be easier to mate with them) and have implied that other men are interested in them as a way of rousing protective jealousy in their partners. For both men and women, the list could go on and on. Even unintelligent men and women possess the same keen ability to develop and implement very complex deceptive strategies with their partners: a compelling argument for the evolutionary psychologists' canon that our brains are "circuited" to achieve certain things and operate on a subconscious level in order to do so.

> ## HOW MEN MISREPRESENT THEMSELVES
>
> Studies have identified some very specific ways in which men misrepresent themselves in order to show women that they are viable potential mates. Among the most common are displays of wealth, excessive acts of kindness, and affection toward children. It's all enough to make you believe the evolutionary psychologists' statements that women are attracted to men who appear to offer support to women's potential offspring.

■ *Vanity and self-alteration.* This is really an extension of deception, mentioned just above. When men and women dye their hair and wear sexy clothing, they are certainly intending to elicit a sexual response on the part of current and prospective sexual partners. (Sometimes, from their *past* sexual partners too!) Yet reproductive psychologists tell us that when humans fuss about their looks, they are really trying to demonstrate their reproductive potential to prospective partners. The woman who wears rouge, lipstick, and vivid makeup is subconsciously trying to demonstrate to males that she is young and endowed with the good blood circulation that places her squarely in her viable reproductive years. The woman who wears a padded bra, gets breast implants, or wears clothing that calls attention to her breasts, similarly, is broadcasting the message that she is reproductively capable and able to nurse. (It is hard to remember that female breasts, despite their vaunted place in our culture and the role they have played in the success of *Playboy* and countless film careers, first existed to nurse young.)

And what about men's vanity and self-misrepresentation? Revealing male clothing sends a signal that the man is ready for reproductive exploits. *Expensive* male clothing sends an additional alert that the man is secure and a good provider. This might well explain the differing standards by which men and women judge the "sexiness" of clothing. On a man, an expensive blue suit with a starched white shirt is something many women find sexy. The same kind of formal business outfit on a woman is rarely seen as sexy to most men, who need to see something of the woman's shape, breasts, legs, and skin in order to become aroused.

Consider too the different, sexually differentiated signals that expensive jewelry sends. When a man flashes an expensive watch and cuff links, he is sending out a sexually charged signal that he is powerful, He can be relied upon as the source of good dinners, good maintenance, and a good inheritance. Yet expensive jewelry on a woman generally sends the opposite signal: she is already in the care of a wealthy, secure man, or so successful in her own right that she doesn't need one. This is a sexist double standard, to be sure. But the fact remains that expensive jewelry generally does not increase a woman's sexual attractiveness (ads to the contrary), even if she was wealthy enough to buy it herself. Women often buy jewelry to reward themselves; men buy it to make a statement about their wealth, status, or sexual attractiveness. The fact that those statements are unpleasant to think about does not mean, sadly, that they might not be true.

THE "BAIT AND WAIT" STRATEGY

Have you noticed that younger professional men and women tend to engage in short-term relationships early in their working years, then become more ready to settle down and get married when age thirty looms on the horizon?

Evolutionary psychologists would tell us that the men are waiting until they have enough power to attract the most desirable partners, and that the women are waiting to select a man who seems to be most stable and best able to provide a secure environment for them and their children.

A SOCIETY OF SEXUAL DOUBLE STANDARDS

If there is truth in these dualisms, we are better able to perceive the supporting structure that lies beneath so many of the double standards that are applied to men and women by many societies today. Here are just a few random examples:

■ A *man who has promiscuous sex with many partners is a "stud."* A woman who does the same thing is a "slut" or "damaged goods."

■ A *man who continues to be promiscuous into his later years is enchanting, like Picasso* (as long as he is not unattractive, lecherous, or completely unsuccessful in his attempts to secure sexual partners, in which case he is branded a "dirty old man"). Women who openly maintain a healthy level of sexual interest into their later years, if you can find them at all, get spoofed on *Benny Hill* and sitcoms. We have no categories for them, except comic ones. From the reproductive point of view in evolution, they have no specific value because they can no longer reproduce.

■ A *wealthy, independent woman is seen as intimidating to prospective mates.* A wealthy independent man may be intimidating to rival men, but he is usually very attractive to women.

■ *Hard-driving businessmen are often seen as sexy and attractive.* Hard-driving businesswomen are "masculine" and sexually ambiguous.

■ *Back in the 1970s, bored couples in the upscale suburbs made the news by holding "wife-swapping parties."* Apparently nobody thought of calling them "husband-swapping parties." 'Nuff said.

■ A *successful businesswoman who supervises many other women is called a "queen bee."* A man who supervises lots of other men is termed an inspiring "leader."

■ *When a highly wealthy, successful woman is courted by a younger man, he is usually perceived to have questionable intentions or morals.* The word *gigolo* sometimes comes into play. Yet when an established older male is courted by a younger woman, everyone "gets it." We have distinct categories, differentiated by sex, for the players in all these complex dramas.

■ *Dumb men are not sexually attractive.* They generally do not offer as much security to women as their smarter counterparts do. Yet women who are dumb, or who feign dumbness, are often highly attractive to men. As we noted earlier, even smart women may sometimes feign stupidity in order to increase their attractiveness to men through the classic "bimbo" ploy.

■ A *man who pursues a woman who does not find him attractive is seen as romantic, courageous, and brave,* unless he cannot stop himself from becoming a stalker. A woman who pursues a man for too long is seen as tragic, sad, and hopeless. She is "throwing herself" at him. So we see that persistence is valuated differently for men and women. There is also a possibility that persistence works better for men than it does for women: a man's perceived value can rise when he continues to express his attraction for a woman over time, even after he has been turned down. (When Hector Berlioz, the French composer, was rejected by an actress, he wrote *Symphonie Fantastique* and dedicated it to her. Not long afterward, they married.) A woman who engages in similar behaviors usually sees her attractiveness decline in the eyes of her would-be partner.

Granted, the above stereotypes are becoming more blurred today. We are making social progress and some of the rules they embody have become stretched over the past decades. Yet the fact that they resonate so well with accepted social patterns makes a convincing case for the conclusion that the roles of men and women, as perceived by society, have been strongly colored by reproductive issues surrounding the sexes.

CHAPTER 15

WHY WE BETRAY

A recent research study conducted in China, Pakistan, Uzbekistan and Mongolia by Dr. Chris Tyler-Smith of Oxford University finds that 16 million men (equal to eight percent of men in those areas) possess Y chromosomes characteristic of the house of the Mongol ruler, Genghis Khan. If this is true, it would mean that one-half of one percent of the world's male population could be descended from just one man—and not a man who lived at the time of Adam and Eve, but as recently as the 12th century. Even though Khan and his immediate descendants ruled over a vast region for two hundred years and fathered a disproportionate number of children among women they had subjugated, the numbers are staggering nonetheless.

—"A Prolific Genghis Khan, It Seems, Helped People the World," *New York Times*, February 11, 2003

IN ADDITION TO ROBERT WRIGHT, another "celebrity" evolutionary psychologist is Dr. David M. Buss, professor of psychology at the University of Michigan. Although certain of his views and research methods have recently come under vigorous attack from rival genetic psychologists, he has achieved popularity with both general readers and academicians through his many books on evolutionary psychology, including *Evolutionary Psychology: The New Science of the Mind, The Evolution of Desire: Strategies of Human Mating,* and *The Dangerous Passion: Why Jealousy Is as Necessary as Love and Sex.*

Of these books, the most germane to our exploration of the Othello response is *The Dangerous Passion*, with its focus on jealousy, betrayal, and violence that result from acts of infidelity. Here are Buss's own words from chapter 1: "At the center of The Dangerous Passion is an exploration of a hazardous region of human sexuality—the desires people experience for those who are not their regular partners and the jealous shield designed to combat its treacherous consequences."

Buss is an accomplished researcher and scientist in his own right. He has read all the pertinent scientific literature about mating and loving relationships, and also conducted studies of his own involving thousands of individuals. *The Dangerous Passion* presents the results of his

HOW WOMEN AND MEN TALK ABOUT MATING

When women talk to other women about their interactions with men, they tend to be consensus-builders. They review dates and conversations with their suitors, asking other women to comment and offer suggestions for appropriate mating strategies.

"Make him wait," "Date other people," or "Now's the time to make him commit" are three common strategies.

When men talk to other men about parallel situations, they are more likely to start with a discussion of whether or not sex occurred and then go on to other topics in descending order of importance. In psycho-evolutionary terms, it may be because by implying that they are having sex with a woman, or *about* to do so, they drive away potential rivals.

work over a span of more than twenty years. The most fundamental question Buss wants us to consider is this: How do men
feel when their partners cheat on them? How do women feel?

In Buss's most famous and controversial study, men and
women were asked to imagine that they had arrived home and
discovered their partners in bed, having sexual relations with
other partners. When men were asked to imagine this scenario, they consistently reported that the thing they would
find most distressing was the fact that their partners were actually *having sex*. Women experienced far different feelings.
They were most distressed by the idea that their men were
establishing close *emotional bonds* with other women. Buss
tells us that this pattern of response remained consistent
among respondents from the United States, the Netherlands,
Germany, Japan, Korea, and Zimbabwe. Lately, other psychologists have conducted surveys that refute Buss's finding by
showing that women also feel distraught by the sexual infidelity of their mates as well as the emotional. Yet to date,
Buss's data and findings remain the most convincing. At the
very least, they offer tremendous food for thought.

Buss tells us that when sexual betrayal takes place, men are
apt to fixate on the sexual aspect of the betrayal and become
violent. In contrast, women want to know, "Do you love her?"
or "Will you continue to see her?" Buss, like Wright, tells us
that these reactions are "hardwired" into our brains.

Why the difference between men and women? Buss concludes that "from an ancestral man's perspective, the single
most damaging form of infidelity his partner could commit, in
the currency of reproduction, would have been a sexual infidelity. A woman's sexual infidelity jeopardizes a man's confidence that he is the genetic father of her children."

Regarding women, he concludes that "our ancestral mothers confronted a different problem, the loss of a partner's commitment to a rival woman and her children. Because emotional involvement is the most reliable signal of this disastrous loss, women key in on cues to a partner's feelings for other women."

> ## ON MEN AND RESOURCES . . .
>
> "There are a number of mechanical devices which increase sexual arousal, particularly in women. Chief among these is the Mercedes-Benz 380SL convertible."
> —P. J. O'Rourke

Men and women are generally not aware of these profound differences in the way jealousy takes hold of them. (You will recall Principle #3 from the evolutionary psychologists at Santa Barbara, noted in the previous chapter: "Consciousness is just the tip of the iceberg. Most of what goes on in our minds is hidden from us.") Like other traits we have inherited though evolutionary natural selection, they have become part of brain circuitry and operate largely on a subconscious level. Buss concludes that men generally have violent tendencies after being betrayed, while women are more likely to feel hurt and betrayed.

Beyond the issue of feelings, Buss shares some other interesting and controversial conclusions about men, women, and sexual infidelity:

- *Men and women have affairs, but generally for different reasons.* As already noted, men may have been "circuited" to spread their genetic material among the largest number of potential offspring. Women may tend to do so for more complex reasons: to have those sexual "backups" in place in the event that the primary relationship goes away, but also to enjoy the resources or emotional sustenance of additional men. However, a cruel double standard is at work here, since women who "stray" are at an astronomically high risk of being harmed by their first partners. Although women do sometimes act violently toward "wandering" males and their partners, women who engage in affairs do so at a far higher risk of violent retribution from their men.

■ *Both men and women have evolved a highly effective system of "signal detection" that often alerts them to the presence of sexual interlopers.* This is one reason why men and women who are prone to jealousy often conjure up fantasies based on false signals that their partners are having affairs. (Remember Desdemona's handkerchief in *Othello*?) Yet there is another troubling truth to consider: a lot of the time, when partners sense the presence of a sexual trespasser, they turn out to be right. In fact, when a relationship dissolves because of one partner's fears that his or her partner is having an extramarital affair with a specific outsider, that very outsider is often the next lover or spouse to step in and occupy a place in the discarded mate's pecking order.

THE PUSH AND PULL OF SEXUAL TIMETABLES

It's truly a "tale as old as time." Men, possibly driven by their evolutionary need to impregnate as many women as possible and spread their genes, seek nearly instantaneous sexual union with the women they pursue. In contrast, a far greater number of women want to let weeks and months pass before agreeing to have sex. Evolutionary psychologists tell us this is because women want to be sure their intended mates are reliable, truthful, healthy, and likely to stay around long enough to provide security both for them and for any offspring that may result.

WHY ARE SOME WOMEN PROMISCUOUS?

If men profit genetically from being promiscuous, why are some women promiscuous too? Why do they choose to have sex with multiple males when they are only capable of bearing offspring sired by one man at any given time? According to evolutionary psychologist David M. Buss, writing in his book *The Dangerous Passion*, the explanation is that cultivating access to numerous male partners was valuable to women in ancient times. Men were likely to die young, often of injuries sustained in conflict or hunting. (Archaeological finds confirm that ancient men were extremely likely, and women extremely unlikely, to die as a result of injuries they got in such activities.) Having other men to serve as "fallbacks" enabled our ancestral women to continue mating during their reproductive years and to pass their genetic material down to succeeding generations, an activity that the evolutionary psychologists tell us is the creative force behind our mating patterns.

While such access to multiple male partners may seem archaic today, studies tell us that when even monogamous marriages or close love partnerships dissolve, women are most likely to forge new love relationships with men they already know: old sweethearts, male friends from the community. If a husband's jealousy spurred the dissolution of the first relationship, they are actually quite likely to take up with the male who was the catalyst for the first husband's jealousy, even if no relationship was actually present before!

Often the signs that a partner has betrayed are clear and easily recognizable: the stereotypical "lipstick on the collar," the new bank accounts suddenly opened in a spouse or partner's name, the unexplained calls on the monthly phone bill.

Yet from his research, Buss concludes that people are often able to tell that a transgression has taken place even when such clear signs are not present. Again, many of our abilities to sense the presence of a sexual "outsider" seem to function at the subconscious level. Real problems can occur when this ability begins to run haywire and a jealous partner, with an attitude approaching paranoia, perceives signs of sexual intrusion where none exist. (When a husband talks to a woman who lives nearby, for example, that's a sure sign that he is having an affair with her. When a girlfriend wears a particular blouse a man has said he likes, that's proof that she is also wearing it to please another man.) Left unchecked, such imaginings make life a living hell and destroy relationships.

Jealousy of our partners has been useful in our evolutionary past. It helped our ancestors deal with a variety of "reproductive threats," such as sexual rivals. "Sexual jealousy is often a successful, although sometimes explosive, solution to persistent predicaments that each one of our ancestors was forced to confront," Buss concludes.

The problem comes when jealousy becomes not only a call to vigilance or to displays of affection to keep a mate from straying, but when it turns obsessive, violent, and destructive. Jealousy, while it may have proven useful for evolutionary purposes, becomes destructive when it misfires and goes awry. Buss points out that nearly all women who enter shelters for battered women state that their partners beat them because they were jealous. Often, these women make statements revealing that their husbands' vigilance, protectiveness, or fear of sexual competitors had become extreme.

Women have entered into relationships with men who engage in obsessive behaviors such as:

- *Obsessively checking up on activities, whereabouts, and friends.* Jealous people follow their partners, hire private investigators, ask friends to confirm their observations and suspicions.

THE AGE DIFFERENTIAL

At the age of twenty-one, men prefer women who are, on average, 2.5 years younger than themselves. As they age, this differential grows. By the time men are in their fifties, they are interested in women who are twenty years younger than they are.

Source: "Age Preferences in Mates Reflect Sex Differences in Reproductive Strategies," by D. T. Kenrick and R. C. Keefe, *Behavioral and Brain Sciences*, vol. 15 (1992)

- *Trying to keep their partners hidden away at home by trying to limit contact with family, friends, etc.* For the "prisoner" partner, life can become a living hell of seclusion in which staying at home is the only way to prevent a partner's accusations or violence.

- *Seizing upon flimsy bits of evidence — real or fabricated — as justification for their obsessive jealousy.* Some obsessively jealous individuals fan the flames of their jealousy by believing that their partners, even if they are going to work or the supermarket, are really sneaking off to have sex with other people. Others seize upon physical evidence or happenstance (a cigarette butt in the driveway, a phone that rings twice but no more) as sure documentation of their partners' infidelities. When Shakespeare had Iago use a flimsy handkerchief to prove Desdemona's treachery, he was tapping into a fundamental psychological truth.

■ *Becoming obsessed with the issues of paternity.* Men who are prone to obsessive jealousy sometimes start to obsess because their children do not look like them. In extreme cases, men have demanded DNA tests to prove that the children in their home are their own; when wives have refused to allow such tests, their suspicious husbands see that as further proof of betrayal, and violence can result.

HOMOSEXUAL MEN AND LESBIANS WANT SOMETHING *ELSE*

In 1984, two psychologists conducted a study of eight hundred personals ads placed by male and female heterosexuals and ads placed by male homosexuals and lesbians. It remains a landmark study to this day, telling us that:

■ Lesbians mention their physical attractiveness in ads only 30 percent of the time, as opposed to 69.5 percent of heterosexual women.

■ Women of both sexual orientations care less about prospective mates' appearance than do men. In ads, only 19.5 percent of heterosexual women and 18 percent of lesbians say they are seeking attractive partners. In contrast, 53.5 percent of male homosexuals and 42.5 percent of heterosexual men say they are seeking partners who are physically attractive.

We can only conclude that men of all stripes are more concerned with the physical beauty of their partners than are any women.

Source: "Courtship in the Personal Column: The Influence of Gender and Sexual Orientation," by K. Deaux and R. Hanna, *Sex Roles*, vol. II (1984)

- *Insulting a woman's intelligence or appearance.* The goal (whether understood by the perpetrator, or operating on the subconscious level) is to lower the woman's self-esteem and make her less likely to believe she is capable of attracting other sexual partners.

- *Succumbing to violent fantasies.* Research shows that violent fantasies are quite common among both men and women who suffer from jealousy. These may become quite intense in the aftermath of breakups with a former partner. Fortunately, only a small percentage of people who have violent fantasies act them out.

- *Finally, engaging in violence.* "Jealousy is the leading cause of spousal battering, " Buss writes, "but it's even worse than that. Men's jealousy puts women at risk of being killed." Statistically, the women most likely to be attacked or killed by their men are those who 1) are considerably younger than their husbands, and 2) have children from previous marriages or relationships. But we need to bear in mind that not only men attack their partners or their partners' real or imagined lovers. Buss tells stories of women who have attacked their rivals with knives, thrown acid in their faces, and exacted other horrible revenges against them.

THE GOOD FACE OF JEALOUSY

Yet Buss hastens to point out that such sensational manifestations of jealousy—the spousal beatings, paranoia, divorces, and so on—are only the most visible and negative results of jealousy in men and women. In the larger scheme of things, Buss reminds us that jealousy may actually be a positive component

HOW MEN AND WOMEN KEEP SEXUAL COMPETITORS AWAY

When you see a man and a woman walking hand in hand, you're apt to think, "Isn't that sweet?" Sweet it may be, but it may also be an overt display of affection designed to keep possible competitors at bay. It's only one ploy people use to keep sexual interlopers away from their partners. Here are some others:

- *Vigilance.* Many men and women are vigilant enough to stay attuned for any signs that a partner's affections may be wandering. *Tactics:* Calling home to see if a partner is there; following a partner; spying on a partner or hiring an investigator to do so; monitoring phone or Internet use; monitoring a partner's behavior at social functions for signs of flirting.

- *Concealing mates. Tactics:* Expecting a partner to remain at home or out of the workforce; refusing to attend social functions where sexual competitors may be present; hiding a partner from friends who might turn out to be competitors; refusing to let a partner engage in social activities with friends of his or her own sex.

- *Engaging in social rituals of commitment. Tactics:* Going steady in high school; exchanging or offering a ring to symbolize that one is "off-limits."

- *Making public displays of affection to communicate a message of exclusivity.* Holding hands in public may appear innocent, but may serve this somewhat clandestine secondary function.

- *Monopolizing.* If you take up all of a partner's time, he or she will simply not have the time to find another lover, or to be found by one. *Tactics:* Going steady in high school; booking all of a partner's time on weekends. Interestingly, this mechanism serves as the downfall of many new relationships, particularly among young couples. One partner quickly backs off from the relationship in order to reconnect with his or her own identity, often using the accurate characterization of "needing more time" before committing to a serious relationship.

of love relationships, provided its obsessive, violent aspects can be held in check. "Although jealousy sometimes can reach pathological or deadly extremes," he writes, "the vast majority of jealous episodes are useful expressions of effective coping strategies that are designed to deal with real threats to relationships."

THE PURPOSE OF LETTER SWEATERS

In nature, many male animals leave a personal scent on or around their mating partners in order to discourage sexual competitors from approaching them. Similar customs exist in high school rituals of going steady, in which the committed partners exchange rings—or in which the female begins to wear a sweater given to her by her partner: a sweater that is ornamented with the letter that the male earned for participation in a varsity sport.

There are few clearer depictions that a female is being protected by a strong male capable of using his physical prowess to defend her from possible rivals. Yet women are not above applying a similar defensive mechanism when they give items of clothing to the lovers in their lives. Could there be an implicit belief that a lover who is wearing such an item of clothing will not sexually betray the woman who gave it.

He's telling us that despite the fact that jealousy makes the nightly news in appalling ways, it is also present in our day-to-day experience, often exerting a positive effect on our love partnerships. Here are some of the positive gifts of jealousy, often forgotten in light of its many dangers:

■ Jealousy causes us to be attentive to our partners, our children, even our homes.

■ Jealousy reminds us that our partners have a sexual value and attractiveness that we do well to honor and observe. If other people find our partners attractive, shouldn't we too?

■ Jealousy spurs us to be good parents and good providers. If we fall below certain standards, our partners might select other partners instead.

■ Jealousy causes us to remain faithful to our primary partners. It makes us aware of the possible cost of our own betrayal.

■ Jealousy spurs us to remain physically attractive and healthy. It reminds us that if we don't keep clean, well groomed, well dressed, and well exercised, our partners might seek out the affections of other partners.

■ Jealousy can serve as a sexual stimulant because when other suitors pay attention to our partners, we are reminded of their attractiveness too.

WHAT CAUSES DIVORCE: THE TWO I'S

According to a classic and often-cited study of men and women from 160 cultures, the two leading causes of marital dissolution are:

■ Infidelity

■ Infertility

It's enough to make you believe the evolutionary biologists' claims that our decisions to both mate and break up hinge on the reproductive viability and availability of our partners.

Source: "Causes of Conjugal Dissolution: A Cross-Cultural Study" by Laura Betzig, *Current Anthropology*, vol. 30 (1989)

■ Jealousy might even offer a compliment to our partners. Through it, we recognize the fact that although our partners could have chosen to invest their love and sexual interest in countless other partners, they instead chose us.

This is part of the rich palette that jealousy brings to our lives. Is it dangerous? Decidedly so. But when viewed in a nuanced way and respected for the rich palette of emotions it brings to our lives, we come to see that, hardwired or not, jealousy can be a boon as well as a negative factor in our lives.

CHAPTER 16
DARWIN AND BEYOND—
THE NEW FACE OF EVOLUTION

A man's drive to mate with as many women as possible has sometimes been called The Coolidge Effect, for President Calvin
Coolidge. How can that be, when "Cool Cal" was known for his
lack of passion? According to a fable, Coolidge and his first lady
were being given separate tours of a farm. While taking the first
tour, Mrs. Coolidge noticed a rooster who was copulating energetically and told her guide, "Please mention that to the President." Later, when the same guide told the President about the
sexually vigorous rooster, Coolidge asked, "Always with the same
hen?" and the guide answered "Oh, no." Coolidge replied,
"Please tell *that* to Mrs. Coolidge." Perhaps Mr. and Mrs. "Cool
Coolidges" were not so reserved after all.

—reported in *The Evolution of Desire* by David M. Buss
(Basic Books, 1994).

AFTER READING THE PRECEDING two chapters, you are probably ready to accept the idea that evolutionary psychologists
really are "onto something" in their theories of how men and
women mate in patterns that have evolved to preserve their
genetic material. At the risk of engaging in stereotypes, what
else could explain men's demonstrated drive to mate with

226

many partners, or women's overriding instinct to nurture their children?

But evolutionary psychologists have a difficult time convincing us that *everything* we do is "hardwired" into our brains to assure the survival of our DNA. After all, people do things that their theories simply do not explain. They are hard-pressed to explain some very common behaviors that run counter to the notion that our behavior is adaptively driven by genes and DNA:

- *Homosexuality.* Men sometimes love men and women sometimes love women. End of story! Evolutionary psychologists have tried to explain these truths by advancing theories that a small number of homosexual individuals in societies have been present to provide an alternate system of child care and family support—and that gay people and lesbians exist because they have served such an evolutionary purpose in wider society. In our view, that seems something of a stretch. After all, we profit from Darwin's natural selection when we do things that help pass our genetic makeup to succeeding generations, not engage in acts that help other people win at that game. For this reason, our gay brothers and sisters appear to belong to a non-Darwinian branch of our family, at least regarding sexual preference. They are our brothers and sisters nonetheless, and their presence in our family offers a clue that there might be other realities of human life that do not fit neatly into the evolutionary theories of evolutionary psychologists. We are not all naked apes.

- *Friendship.* Evolutionary theorists say that friendship, which is after all a more common form of human bonding than love, is another adaptive human tendency. They tell us that societies where friendship exists are more cohesive and resistant to outside attack, for instance. We have therefore

OPPOSING OUR DESIRES CAN BE BEAUTIFUL

Plays, novels, and operas sometimes depict people who go against their psycho- evolutionary tendencies and graciously give up their mates to younger or more competitive alternatives.

In all of opera, few moments make tears flow more freely than the moment late in Strauss's opera *Der Rosenkavalier* when the Marschallin, an elegant but aging woman, graciously stands aside and lets her young boyfriend pursue his plans to marry a much younger woman.

It gives us a glimpse into some of the richness of life that can result when we execute the moral control to subjugate our own drives in favor of others.

developed the capacity to be friends. Chimpanzees and bonobos, our closest genetic relatives, have friends too. Evolutionary psychologists also maintain that we have developed the ability to be friends so that backup care providers will tend to our children if we die young. Yet such theorizing falls short when it comes to explaining the human's extraordinary capabilities to enter into close, lifelong friendships. Friendship, that central part of human experience, cannot be fully explained in terms of evolutionary psychology.

■ *Bravery and self-sacrifice.* Sacrificing personal resources and even one's life is not adaptive, yet many of us are willing to do so. Sometimes we act selflessly to help friends, but there are also countless instances of bravery in which one person gives up life itself to protect or save strangers. Soldiers do so in war; firefighters and police officers do so as part of their jobs. Darwinist theories have no category for such self-sacrifice, yet it remains a fact of life.

■ *Suicide.* Why is self-destruction so widespread? It clearly serves no evolutionary purpose. Since the human animal is the only one to commit suicide, the notion of destroying oneself seems to have arrived as a by-product of human intelligence, not evolution from lower primates. It's therefore not illogical to conclude that humans have developed other abilities and tendencies (both good and bad) that serve no evolutionary purpose. Fidelity comes to mind.

■ *Infanticide.* It's horrible to think about. Yet the fact remains that when men become violently jealous and take revenge on women for real or perceived infidelities, they often take the lives of their own children, destroying their own genetic material. We also need to confront the reality that women sometimes kill their own children too. We remember that in 2001, a woman named Andrea Yates killed her five children. It was a horrible act that made national news, perhaps due to the fact that her actions were not only horrible, but counter to her own genetic self-interest.

Our evolutionary psychologist friends can explain many things about the way we behave, but they cannot explain *everything*. Human beings, in fact, have a broad spectrum of passions and drives that have not been influenced at all by the forces of natural or sexual selection. We nurture, teach, and cherish other people's children. We sometimes forgive

EXERCISE: LOOK AT YOUR REPUDIATED PASSIONS FROM A DARWINIST PERSPECTIVE

Many of us have learned to deny the drives that we know to be immoral or "not nice." In fact, whole religions have been built upon the notion that we can achieve spiritual growth only by denying our carnal impulses.

We're certainly not suggesting that you discover your darker desires and act on them. But at the same time, uncovering and examining them from the perspective of evolutionary psychologists can lead to a greater self-understanding and even a more successful relationship with those we love.

You need not tell other people about the darker things you find in your mental "locker." This is a private exercise. But instead of repudiating desires and driving them back, consider bringing them out into the open where you can examine them objectively.

Much as you might not like to admit it, you might find you're harboring desires and drives like these:

- When you are out with your spouse, you really do enjoy flirting with other people.

- You like to dress provocatively as a way to hold the interest of your primary partner.

- When you see your partner speaking with an attractive "outsider," you experience emotions you do not like—a tendency to act violently, to become upset, to flirt with someone to "get back" and tip the balance in your favor.

- Even though you are in a stable relationship, you're having sexual fantasies about some of the people at work.

- Even though you're "happily married," you subscribe to provocative magazines and keep a stack of them hidden away.

- While you are having sex with your partner, you sometimes pretend that he or she is someone else.

- You've developed an obsessional crush on someone who is not your spouse or usual partner.

Be gentle on yourself as you bring these repudiated desires into the open. Examine them objectively, intellectually, without passion, and—if you can manage it—without self-justification ("My husband has gotten fat. Why shouldn't I look at other men!") or defensiveness ("Millions of men rent X-rated movies. It's not abnormal!").

Chances are that you will discover that some of the drives and desires you have been feeling spring from evolutionary "hardwiring" we have discussed— the desire for sexual variety, for example, or the tendency to be protective and possessive of your spouse. Such discoveries, if freely admitted, can have a liberating effect on our relationships, allowing us to own up to emotions such as, "I see that my genes and instincts are ordering me to have sex with thousands of partners, but I choose to stay with just one. Isn't it funny that I still feel these hereditary drives?"

Other discoveries may not be so positive or easy to shrug off and may serve as important indicators of areas in your relationships that need attention and possibly the assistance of a qualified therapist. For the sake of your own health, the well-being of your partner and the overall success of your love relationship, you need to bring such drives as these out into the light of day:

- Fantasies of using physical violence against your partner, members of your family, or anyone else.

- Engaging in excessive vigilance or surveillance of your partner in order to keep him or her from establishing ties with anyone else.

- Intentionally trying to lower your partner's feelings of self-esteem or attractiveness so he or she will not "wander."

- Trying to "hide" your partner by refusing to attend social events outside the home.

The things you discover in your "Darwin Inventory" might not all be happy discoveries, or easy things to accept about yourself. Having the courage to bring them into the open can be a vital first step toward building better relationships and insulating your life from the damaging effects of the Othello response.

infidelities. We honor our departed parents and relatives. We listen to Mozart and visit art museums. We read books. On and on the list goes.

Yet most people, when encountering evolutionary psychologists and their beliefs, succumb to a certain feeling of implied inevitability. They come to believe that their "hardwired" behavior patterns are blueprints for future behavior that is all but inevitable. We have heard this conclusion lurking beneath statements like these:

> ### THE OTHELLO RESPONSE AND MURDER
>
> A full 13 percent of all homicides are spousal murders, and jealousy is the leading cause.

- "As a man, I'm genetically programmed to chase lots of women. The evolutionary psychologists prove that I'm all but sure to do it. It's out of my control."

- "As a woman about to pass beyond my childbearing years, I am about to become unattractive to my husband. In fact, to all men."

- "I'm a man who will never earn a lot of money. Since women want men with vast resources to provide for them, I will probably have a hard time retaining my wife's affections."

- "I become insanely jealous, to the point of having an impulse to act violently, whenever I see my partner flirting with someone else. It's a natural thing, since I've been programmed to have these violent thoughts, maybe even act violently, through millions of years of human evolution. It's beyond my control."

The fallacy of these outlooks is the belief that we are powerless to control the impulses nature gave us to help assure that we will procreate successfully. Do we really have no control over violent, immature, or nearly paranoid behaviors? Can't we sometimes remind ourselves that our "inner voices" are issuing instructions we should not obey: signals that, although strong, really represent choices that are immoral, immature, or destructive. In other words, we have the option to give in to our evolutionary "hardwiring," or step back and exert control over ourselves, using our higher mind.

Some of us are able to behave in better ways, despite our tendencies. People who behave in just this kind of moral way are all around us. (Hopefully, we are members of their ranks!) They do not betray their lovers. They do not become violent when jealousy or insecurity strikes. These moral people do not make the evening news because they don't kill people. They don't make tabloid headlines because they don't sleep around. They are simply people who own their capacity to behave morally—often exhibiting behavior that runs contrary to the way evolutionary psychologists tell us we are "programmed" to act. And even though we might not be able to name them at first, they are all around us, and their faces are familiar enough after all:

- A high school teacher discovers that a handsome young male student has a crush on him and he can't deny that he is complimented and excited. But he also realizes the emotional damage he could inflict by entering into a relationship with the young man. He takes the higher road and serves as a mentor and friend—someone the young student can come back to visit in the years ahead as he moves forward through life. He is taking the higher road away from self-gratification and making a positive difference in someone else's life.

■ A woman who lives in an affluent suburb of New York remains strongly supportive of her husband despite the fact that he has seen two businesses fail and suffered severe financial hardship. Her decision to do so runs against the social conventions of her social circle. In fact, friends whose husbands are experiencing periods of success are pressuring her to "start looking for a man who can support her in the style she deserves." Yet she recalls her marriage vows, supports her husband, suggests that they sell her old Mercedes that's sitting in the garage, and starts a job search of her own. Is she frustrated? Definitely. But she has also determined that she has the option to take the higher road.

SEX ON THE FIRST DATE

Five percent of women say it's okay to have sex on a first date, compared with 33 percent of men. Moral: If you don't want to have sex on the first date, don't date a man!

Source: A poll of twenty-five hundred men and women conducted by *Divorce Magazine*, May 2002

■ A married man is powerfully drawn to a young female colleague who just joined his company. The strength of his infatuation nearly astounds him. He cannot stop thinking about what it would be like to make a sexual advance toward her, to go away for the weekend with her, to have sex with her. Yet he counterbalances his new obsession with rational thoughts about what would happen to him and his family if he allowed all that to happen. He would destroy his happy, long-standing marriage to a woman he loves. He would severely damage the happiness of his two young children. He also is mature enough to realize that any affair with the young woman would probably be short-lived, as were the affairs he had before he and his wife got married. He realizes that he is only engaging in a common fantasy of many aging men: the notion that a younger woman would welcome sexual advances instead of seeing them as harassment. He sees he has the power to direct and shape his own life with his intellect and moral sense—not be a slave to his brain or his hormones.

■ After a man learns that his former girlfriend is now seeing someone else, he cannot stop all the odd and violent fantasies that course through his mind. He considers sitting in his car outside her building so he can see her and her new lover when they enter or leave. He thinks about calling her number to see if her new lover answers. He imagines running into her and her new boyfriend in a restaurant and envisions the violent fight that results when he confronts his "rival" and beats him publicly. Yet even though these fantasies exert a powerful pull, he realizes that he can control himself and do what is right. He can make the decision to let his former lover live her life. He can have the courage to start over again in a new relationship of his own! If he ever runs into his former girlfriend and her new man, he can just say hello graciously and maturely. After all, he's not a caveman! Is he?

On and on the examples could go. You could doubtless find similar examples in your own past: times when you heard the call of ancient impulses, but decided that you could exercise the more evolved parts of your brain to behave as you decided, not as you were hardwired to do.

WHAT KINSEY TOLD US ABOUT MEN WHO VISIT PROSTITUTES . . .

Viewed from the perspective of evolutionary psychology that men need to "spread their seed" among many females, the reasons for male promiscuity become clear. It also becomes clearer why some men visit prostitutes in order to satisfy their drive for sex with multiple partners. How many American men visit prostitutes? Is it a recent phenomenon, due to a recent decline in morals? Apparently not.

Let's go back to the granddaddy of all sex surveys, *Sexual Behavior in the Human Male*, a study of twelve thousand American men conducted by Alfred Charles Kinsey in 1948. Kinsey found that "about 69 percent of the total white male population ultimately has some experience with prostitutes . . . something between 3.5 and 4 percent of the total outlet of the male population (single and married) is drawn from relations with female prostitutes." Kinsey then documents at great length how and when men have their contacts with prostitutes: younger men were more apt to do it, single men, less educated men, etc.

It's an old study, but its figures are staggering all the same. These words from Kinsey shed light on the underlying reason why such a large percentage of men seek sex for pay: "At all social levels men go to prostitutes because it is simpler to secure a sexual partner commercially than it is to secure a sexual partner by courting a girl who would not accept pay."

Source: *Sexual Behavior in the Human Male*, by Alfred Charles Kinsey, 1948

We'd like to coin a new name for this kind of moral behavior. We'd like to call it "Riding Darwin's Bike."

RIDING DARWIN'S BICYCLE

Why can people ride bicycles? After all, riding a bicycle is a very complicated activity. It involves keen coordination of vision with many physical actions, including steering, pedaling, and shifting weight to maintain balance.

It would appear to be a skill that required millions of years for people to develop. Lots of brain circuits would need to be hardwired, certainly many more than are involved in the process of walking, which took our forbears millions of years to achieve. Additionally, we wouldn't be surprised to hear that millions of our ancestors perished in the attempt to learn to ride bicycles. It's logical. We must be the lucky people who succeeded in the evolutionary, Darwinian game of natural selection that led to our ability to ride two-wheelers.

Yet that line of logical reasoning is completely wrong. Bicycles and bicycle-like devices have been around for less than two centuries. They have been in widespread use for only about one hundred years. In fact, human evolution had nothing to do with the fact that people learned to ride bikes. No matter where we look, we won't find any archaeological digs alongside our highways where we can study the bones of unsuccessful bicycle riders who perished in their evolutionary quest to ride upright on two wheels.

Yet the question is: How can we manage to perform such a complex task as bicycle riding when we have had no specific programming for it over the millennia? And while we're at it, why are we able to walk tightropes, become competitive divers, drive cars, play the piano, or engage in so many other complicated tasks for which we have no specific preparation through the forces of selective adaptation?

The answer is quite simple. Riding a bicycle, or performing any one of those other complex tasks, is an activity that is built upon other brain functions, physical abilities, and skills that have been cultivated in us over the course of evolution. We can balance on a speeding bicycle because our keen balancing skills have already been evolved through millennia of walking and running. We can pedal bicycles because we have already evolved very strong leg muscles for locomotion, not to mention the mental "hardware" to operate them. We have the stamina to ride long distances on bikes because evolution equipped us with strong lungs needed for strenuous running and hunting. We use visual cues to guide our bicycles safely because our highly acute vision systems adapted gradually to help us hunt and avoid danger.

So we see that we can master, coordinate, and finally exceed our innate abilities and tendencies. We are not slaves to them. We don't need to use them only in old ways (fighting, hunting, climbing high hills after our prey) that might no longer serve us. We can tap into them and utilize them in new and often astonishing ways.

We can utilize this opportunity in our relationships too. Like the people we discovered above (the man who is attracted to a young lover but who chooses to behave morally, the woman who is frustrated by economic hardship but who chooses not to punish her husband), we have the opportunity to control what we do and how we behave. Evolution, through some miracle that is yet to be understood, has made us not only into animals — but also into animals who can behave morally.

Even in the direst moments when our despair overtakes us, another path is open before us as an alternative to violence. We can turn away from the harm we are about to do, step back, and choose a better course of action. Unlike the ancient ancestors that Darwin described, who had no choice but to act violently in the world, we have reasoning minds and other alternatives. As modern people, we are free to act in modern ways.

CHAPTER 17

CONFRONTING OUR WRATH

A 22-year-old aspiring actress whose former fiancé harassed her for two months before shooting her in the face and killing himself outside her Lower East Side apartment building early Thursday morning, died at Bellevue Hospital Center yesterday, the authorities said.

The woman, Lyric Benson, who graduated from Yale last year and worked as a hostess at the SoHo brasserie Balthazar while performing voice-overs and appearing in soap operas and advertisements, was shot outside her building at 211 East Broadway by Robert J. Ambrosino, 32, the police said.

—"Young Actress Shot by Former Fiancé Dies,"
by Robert D. McFadden,
New York Times, April 26, 2003

ALTHOUGH IT MIGHT SEEM like a curious topic to bring up in a modern, therapeutically oriented book on obsessive jealousy, let's turn our attention to a topic that appears ancient and out of synch with the way people think and act today. It is the concept of *sin*.

In medieval Europe, most people could recite from memory a short list of the Seven Deadly Sins. More than just a list of forbidden activities, they were a part of the common conception of the way the world, and human experience, could be understood.

The Seven Deadly Sins were:

- Pride

- Envy

- Wrath

- Sloth

- Avarice

- Gluttony

- Lechery (also called lust)

We don't stop to think about them often today. Some of us encounter them when we see the stark images that Heironymus Bosch, the Dutch painter and printmaker, created for each of them. And we sometimes encounter them in literary works, such as *The Book of the Courtier* by Baldesar Castiglione, an Italian renaissance treatise about proper courtly behavior. Castiglione dealt with the sins and their effects on both proper manners and, by extension, the inner world we create for ourselves.

THE CONCEPT OF SIN

So what is sin all about? Is it an old, restrictive concept we can discard at the side of the road with our other discarded cultural artifacts? Perhaps we can. After all, only some religions and denominations talk a great deal about sin today. Many people seem to be doing a fine job of living morally and well without turning our attention to the idea.

Yet before we do that, it might prove useful to give the issue a little consideration. Why did sin hold such

> **MEN ENGAGE IN MORE SEXUAL FANTASIES THAN WOMEN DO**
> Comparison studies in the United States, Japan, and Great Britain all conclude that men's sexual fantasies occur with twice the frequency as women's.
>
> Source: "Sex Differences in Sexual Fantasy: An Evolutionary Psychological Approach," by B. J. Ellis and D. Symons, *Journal of Sex Research*, vol. 27 (1990)

a central place in the thinking of our Western cultural forebears only one thousand years ago? Is it logical to think that sin, which so recently was central to Western thought, quietly "exited stage right" from our world and timidly left our way of thinking?

We believe sin is worth thinking about, not as part of the "If I do something wrong, I go to hell" equation, but because we believe that understanding sin can teach us important lessons about what it means to live effectively, even today.

BEYOND BEING NAUGHTY OR NICE

In the classical conception, sin really means the antitheses of virtue. We also know that the classical Greek word for sin was Homartia. It was not only a word for sin. It also was an archery term that meant *missing the mark*. So we see that, in the classical mind, we are simply off course in our lives when we fall victim to the Seven Deadly Sins. When we become involved in sin, we allow our lives to be pulled away from where we

ought to be going. We turn our backs on what is good in ourselves and what we have the potential to achieve.

Where are our going when we let Homartia take us over
and cause us to miss the target? Perhaps the answer lies in the
writing of Saint Thomas Aquinas, who made this observation
about sin: "Sin is misdirected love." In this thought, we find
a kernel of truth about each of the Seven Deadlies. Each of
the sin categories they represent can be seen as good love
gone awry:

- Pride is self-belief and self-awareness that has become per-
  verted into self-love.

- Envy is loving admiration for others that has been turned
  inside out and directed against ourselves.

- Wrath is healthy anger that has become uncontrolled and
  obsessive.

- Sloth is the healthy need for relaxation, self-care, and
  "recharging," taken to unhealthy extremes.

- Avarice is a drive for material security that has been allowed
  to turn to obsessive greed.

- Gluttony is healthy love of self-nourishment gone terribly
  awry.

- Lechery is a need for love and physical intimacy that has
  become obsessive, and distorted, and self-destructive.

Sin as an Invitation to the Othello Response

The Seven Deadly Sins, if allowed to take hold in our lives, can form a fertile breeding-ground for the Othello response. There is no better way to glimpse this reality than to review the way that several of the Seven Deadlies function to undo Othello in the Othello play:

- Othello's *pride* makes him want to appear strong and in control of his life and his relationship. When he suspects that Desdemona is having sex with another man, his vanity and pride serve as a major impetus to carry his delusions through to a violent outcome.

- *Envy* plays many roles in the play. Othello envies the younger, native, well-connected Cassio to the point where he is easily convinced that this other man is having sexual relations with his wife.

- *Wrath* and visions of murder take on a life of their own, taking control of Othello and driving him to vengeance.

Of these three, obsessive wrath is the sin that led Othello to cry "Blood!" and smother his innocent wife. And it can surely wreak great harm in our lives. In our lives, too, we invite disaster when we allow obsessive anger and wrath to gain a foothold over us. More than merely sinful, doing so represents an *inefficient* way to live, luring us into a false shadow world — an unreal universe where we are at high risk of taking destructive action against ourselves and those we love.

Let's consider a case study.

Murder on a Wedding Day

On September 26, 1999, in Hackensack New Jersey, a man named Agustin Garcia shot Gladys Ricart, his former girlfriend, as she was having her wedding pictures taken. It was only minutes before she would marry another man. People were shocked. Garcia had been a highly respected community leader across the river in New York, where he had devoted himself to working with young people in his neighborhood.

How could such a "good guy" gun down a lovely young woman whom he claimed to love? Garcia and his lawyer had an explanation. At the trial, they asked whether Garcia could defend himself using a "crime of passion" defense, meaning that he was so jealous that he could not control his actions. The judge agreed and Garcia's attorneys were hopeful that he

A WINE COMMERCIAL THAT MADE US THINK

Back in the early 1990s, television across America aired a charming commercial for Bolla wine that proved to be very popular. It showed a handsome, dapper man of about sixty sitting in an Italian café with a glass of wine in front of him. At a moment he seemed to be anticipating, a very beautiful young woman came walking down the street. Unnoticed by her, he lifted his glass to her in a silent toast.

The story in the vignette was clear. The fact that the man appeared to be waiting for the young woman let us know that he sat there on many days, waiting for her. We know that he was possibly in love with her or, at the very least, enchanted by her beauty. Yet we also know that he was standing on the sidelines without intervening. He was apparently content to let her go on and lead her own life. Perhaps he was living in the memory of his own youth or the memory of some lost love. He was experiencing some bittersweet emotion that we could recognize and share.

It was just a commercial, to be sure. But it served as a reminder that we often enjoy more of the richness of life, even enjoying its sadness, when we understand our instincts yet temper them with a higher moral sense.

would be convicted on a lesser charge of manslaughter. Yet it didn't work, and Garcia is now in jail, a convicted murderer.

Wrath, once it gains control over us, can do immense harm. Usually the danger is most acute for those who are closest to us. As our lives spin out of control, it is they who are closest to the dangerous and erratic epicenter of our lives.

UNMASKING WRATH

How can you determine whether the seductive power of wrath and the other Seven Deadly Sins might be pulling your relationship off course, leading to baseless suspicions of your partner and other problems that can lead to the Othello response?

It is a question that is best approached indirectly. After all, "Am I living in sin?" can be a very overwhelming (and unfashionable) question to ask. Uncovering the problem is easier if we ask, more simply: Are there anger-flooded areas and issues in your loving relationship? Are there topics you are afraid to touch upon, for fear of your own anger, or that of your partner? Bringing these issues to light is the most efficient way to get a glimpse of the areas where irrational jealousy (and sin, if you will) might have gained a hold over you.

You might find that you have succumbed to chronic anger in areas such as these:

- You remain angry about previous jealousy-inducing events in your relationship, such as a partner's previous flirtations (real or perceived) or previous relationships.

- You are angry with yourself because you are thinking of straying from the relationship. That might sound irrational, but obsessive behavior, by definition, is.

■ You experience unusual rage concerning your partner's involvement with his or her children from a previous marriage or relationship.

LEARNING TO TRUST THAT YOUR PARTNER WILL BE THERE

According to the psychologist Jean Piaget, small children develop object constancy between the ages of two and four. If you hide a ball under a rug, they will be despondent. That ball is gone; it is gone forever! They will not realize that it is just under the rug. Or if Mommy leaves the room, Mommy is really gone! She has gone to Mars or to heaven!

Then over time, children develop object constancy. They no longer need to have something in sight to know that it still exists. Yet many people who suffer from obsessive jealousy apparently lack this basic ability. They lack the ability to know that when their lover or partner is not in sight, he or she has not disappeared for all time.

Part of loving another person is to allow autonomy, realizing that you know and trust him or her. They may have left the house, the town, or the state, but they will return! That level of faith is one of the building blocks of a trusting, durable relationship.

It can be challenging to set our egos aside and consider such questions calmly and objectively. But in the end, our ability to be calm and detached (which often means getting our egos out of the process) can save us from calamitous tendencies, beliefs, and actions.

In practical terms, this means making a commitment to obtain accurate information about what is truly taking place before letting jealousy or anger gain control over you. If we could learn only one lesson from Shakespeare's *Othello*, it ought to be that getting accurate information about what is really taking place in our relationships can save us untold sorrow and harm.

Othello and Desdemona were newlyweds. Othello had very little idea what was truly taking place in Desdemona's life. It was therefore easy for him to accept a false (and possibly "sinful," in the sense of being off the mark) conception of reality that Iago created to destroy him. If Othello had taken the time to investigate, talk with his wife, and understand her true reality, he would never have acted to destroy his wife and his world.

Why did he do it? He was a smart, accomplished human, like us. Can't such people take the time to reject deceptive attitudes—"sinful" outlooks that pull our lives off course—and defeat the "green-eyed monster" of jealousy before it defeats us?

With courage and commitment, we can learn to:

- *Be wary* of the call of jealousy, recognizing it as a powerful force with the power to unleash irreparable harm in our lives.

- *Refuse to accuse our partners* based on inadequate information. Instead of saying, "That other man was coming on to you at the party, wasn't he?" we can step back and say, "I need to understand what I was feeling at the party, and maybe what you were feeling too."

- *Accept appropriate personal responsibility* for our own feelings of anger and jealousy. Instead of blaming our partners when our own feelings of jealousy strike, we can accept some of the onus ourselves. One worthwhile approach is to ask self-assessment questions, such as "Am I overreacting?" and "Is my reaction based on adequate information?"

Case Study: Miriam and Scott

Miriam's husband, Scott, was becoming increasingly withdrawn.

He rarely wanted to attend social functions where other men might be present. It was almost as though Scott wanted to keep her at home, "concealed" and out of the reach of possible competitors for his affection.

One summer weekend the couple did attend a family function—a birthday party that would have been very difficult to avoid. Miriam, who was delighted to have some social interaction with her family, was standing by the barbecue grille chatting with her brother-in-law when Scott threw his drink down onto the deck and stormed away. When Miriam caught up with him in the living room, he was breathing heavily and covered with sweat. He accused Miriam of flirting and demanded that they leave at once.

Miriam was torn apart emotionally by the situation and didn't know what to do. She could proclaim her innocence, like Desdemona, and tell Scott he was out of line. She could tell Scott to go home by himself, delaying a confrontation with him until she arrived home later on. She could insist that Scott apologize to her family for his behavior. Worse yet, he seemed so upset that she could see that he really needed her support. Should she just leave with him and avoid conflict? What kind of precedent would that set?

But before she could decide what to do, Scott began to cry, apologized, and asked to go back into the party. This pattern is not uncommon in obsessively jealous men. Even after extreme emotional actions or reactions, they are prone to say, "It will never happen again," and plead to be forgiven. It's a pattern that, unless addressed, can escalate and lead to a severely dysfunctional relationship, even violence. If Miriam and Scott were our friends, we would encourage Scott to seek counseling—encourage Miriam to seek qualified help too—before the troubling patterns become even worse.

Instead of allowing extreme, irrational emotions to gain power over us, we can choose a reality-seeking path that leads to a more efficient, enlightened way of living. The hidden underlying goal is to love truly—to fully grasp the realities of our loved ones instead of being seduced into thinking about what they do wrong, what they lack, and why they make us angry. The goal of love, after all, is to love. (Let's keep it simple!)

While this might be advocating a passionless, sterile way of living, the opposite is actually the case. When we free ourselves from Pride, Envy, Wrath, and the others, we free ourselves to live—and love—more deeply and fully. We fall in love with what is true and real in our partners, in ourselves, and in our lives. We set our feet upon a path of more fulfilling and evolved life.

MONOGAMY IS NOT EASY

The traditional marital vows written into the *Book of Common Prayer* talk about the difficult aspects of entering into a long-term love bond. These words, commonly recited as part of the marriage ceremony, urge us to become steadfast in our love and look forward to a life together "for better, for worse, for richer, for poorer, in sickness and in health, until we are parted by death."

These word are so realistic, they might even become depressing if we stopped to think about what they have to tell us. They tell us that in a committed long-term relationship, we're going to have to be together though economic situations that will change, when our health will deteriorate—when life gets worse.

In any relationship, life together is certainly going to be rough at times! To keep going through the rough times, we need more than rosy-hued, romantic love. We need to work hard to keep our relationships strong over time.

CHAPTER 18

VIRTUOUS PROTECTION FROM
THE OTHELLO RESPONSE

Virtue! a fig! 'tis in ourselves that we are thus or thus. Our bodies
are our gardens, to the which our wills are gardeners: so that if
we will plant nettles, or sow lettuce, set hyssop and weed up
thyme, supply it with one gender of herbs, or distract it with
many, either to have it sterile with idleness, or manured with
industry, why, the power and corrigible authority of this lies in
our wills. If the balance of our lives had not one scale of reason
to poise another of sensuality, the blood and baseness of our
natures would conduct us to most preposterous conclusions: but
we have reason to cool our raging motions, our carnal stings, our
unbitted lusts, whereof I take this that you call love to be a sect
or scion.

—Iago, speaking of virtue, in *Othello*, Act I, Scene 3

In the medieval mind, there were specific antidotes, strong
enough to protect us from the subverting powers of the the
Seven Deadly Sins. These antidotes were called *Virtues*.

Like the Seven Deadly Sins themselves, the notion of
Virtue seems to have left our contemporary way of thinking.
Today, when we speak of a "virtuous" man or woman, we
rarely touch upon the full significance of what Virtue meant

in ages past. In contemporary life, a "virtuous" person is seen as physically attractive and materially accomplished, possibly someone who has navigated life well and gotten some "good stuff" as a reward.

The respect accorded to Virtue was far greater in the classical world of Aristotle and later in that of Saint Thomas Aquinas as he breathed new life into classical ideas and shaped them into new Christian con-

REGARDING HENRY

The 1991 movie *Regarding Henry* told the story of a hard-driving and very angry attorney named Henry who had a terrible time controlling his temper. Then, when Henry got shot in the head during a holdup, his memory got erased, along with his aggression. By the end of the movie, Henry was a changed man—very kind and loving toward his family.

This is a magic-bullet scenario on curing a relationship. In reality, it takes work and introspection to chase anger out of our lives.

texts. In this older worldview, a virtuous person was someone who had worked long and hard at understanding both him- or herself and the moral demands of living effectively in the real world. The virtuous person, through hard work, had become able to live an accomplished and serene life.

As the cultural historian Josef Pieper reminded us in his extraordinarily revealing books, including and especially *The Four Cardinal Virtues*, Virtue is much more than some kind of enhanced *looking good*. Virtue is something we should still be seeking today. The four classical Virtues Pieper identifies are:

- Prudence

- Justice

- Fortitude

- Temperance

In classic times, they were seen as pathways that, if practiced, led to a more evolved and effective life. Peiper urged modern people to reconsider what Virtue means and to try to return it to the center of Western mores and morality.

VIRTUE VS. THE OTHELLO RESPONSE

On first glance, it might be difficult to understand the tie-in between personal Virtue and the destabilizing force of the Othello response. But then we consider that by elevating yourself by practicing Virtue and making yourself more solid, you develop a stronger, more realistic, and more adult relationship with the world.

Because your world outlook is more solidly grounded in reality, not "sinful" self-deceptions, you are less taken in by the half-truths, faulty assumptions, and immature anger and jealousy that add up to the Othello response.

After all, any love relationship that is founded on jealousy, or permeated by it, can never be an adult relationship. Jealousy-permeated relationships are based on one or more of the following components, which are clearly not virtuous in the classical sense:

> ## VIRTUE REQUIRES PERSISTENCE
>
> Virtue means taking actions in service of expressing your love by doing *things*, by taking responsibility, taking initiative. It means the ability to hang in there when things are tough, remembering what is real and truly understood about your love and your relationship. It also means continuing to take responsibility for the work of love, even when the going gets tough.

SELF-JUSTIFICATION AS AN EXIT STRATEGY

When seeking a way out of a relationship, people often develop self-justifying positions to demonstrate to themselves, and to others, that they were "right" to end the relationship because their partners had done something "wrong."

■ "My husband was so bad with money, I had to get out or go under too," says a woman.

■ "My wife was insanely possessive of me and my time, she was suffocating me, I had to get out of there," a man says.

There are times when relationships should not endure. But often, people fix upon such justifications as mechanisms to end their relationship, without acting to try to correct the problem instead. If your relationship is essentially happy and worth preserving, it is important so ask whether you have tried to rectify your problems, or are simply looking at them as justifications for "getting out" and moving on. If that is what you are doing, you might as well admit it and consider whether it's a course of action you genuinely wish to pursue.

■ A desire to engage in a false and unnecessary process of living rather than a genuine one.

■ An agitated, exaggerated fear of abandonment.

■ A hidden, self-destructive desire to be betrayed, even destroyed.

■ A lack of genuine desire for intimacy.

■ A preference for suspicion and half truth over knowledge and true understanding.

■ A need to divert oneself from what is important in life, what is truly needed.

This is only the start of a very long list, yet when we look at it, it becomes obvious that cultivating Virtue might serve as a very practical antidote to the Othello response. Virtue makes us stronger people, in touch with what is best in ourselves and in others. It puts us in contact with our genuine needs, not false ones based on fear or distorted reality. It leads us to become people who can trust, and are worthy of trust.

Seen in this way, it becomes clear that when we seek and practice Virtue, we tap into a stabilizing and profoundly life-orienting force. Let's take a closer look at the four classical Virtues and the power they have to transform our lives.

THE VIRTUE OF PRUDENCE

Prudence has a unique potential to orient our lives and make us resilient against jealousy and the Othello response. Like the word *Virtue* itself, the word *Prudence* has fallen out of fashion today. It has an aura of irrelevance, like something the Puritans or Pilgrims had on their minds. At best, it sounds like something we left behind on our way to the mall of modern life, something to do with being careful.

Yet then we begin to understand the real meaning of Prudence: the perfected ability to make right decisions and good choices in life. Through Prudence, we become better able to do the right things and act in positive ways, based on reality, not illusions, in the face of complex realities that confront us. Prudence equips us with a moral and clear mind that helps us deal realistically with the conflicts we face in life.

Obviously, such an ability can be very helpful in vaccinating ourselves, and our relationships, against many destabilizing forces. Who among us wouldn't benefit from possessing a virtue like that, especially where love is the issue?

CONSIDERATION: THE FIRST ACT OF PRUDENCE

Consideration is a process we need to engage in *before* we take potentially momentous actions that will have major life consequences. Before we accuse our partners of infidelity or start to have affairs, for example, we stop to consider the actions we are on the verge of taking. The ability to reflect before acting can be a beneficial trait as we go through life, possibly one that is on the wane today.

We also need to bear in mind that just stopping to think before we act is not enough. We also need to cultivate a process of living that anchors us continually in what is true and real in our lives, and that helps us discard what is illusory and false. Saint Thomas Aquinas, in particular, cautioned about the necessity of having a reality-based worldview and of making decisions that are congruent with it: in other words, in line with reality.

If we want an example of a worldview that is not reality-based, we need go no farther than the play *Othello* and the jealous world that the title character constructs to justify the

---

STAYING CENTERED IN REALITY

Prudence and Virtue have a lot to do with staying centered and grounded in reality. We become virtuous when we are constantly in touch with questions like these:

- What's really true?

- Where am I fooling or deluding myself about my love and my life?

- What are the most basic, fundamentally important things to me?

INVITING SPIRITUAL MEANING INTO RELATIONSHIPS

Many people discover a spiritual side to relationships and marriage. Some people see their relationships as "holy places" where both partners can explore the spiritual aspects of being in love with another person, or as places where they can learn and make personal progress by relating closely to another person who is loved.

On a certain level, a relationship can even serve as a mnemonic device, like attending church services on Sunday or lighting candles on Friday night when Shabbat begins. In the quiet and peace of that central relationship, we are able to connect to our spiritual selves and to God in addition to our partners.

murder of his wife. Nothing about that world is rooted in reality. It is all untruth and half-truth. The few shreds of reality that are allowed to permeate it (the handkerchief that Iago convinces Othello has been lost) are skewed and distorted to fit into the landscape of a false, distorted world. It appears probable that Othello could have saved himself, and those around him, simply by practicing Prudence. In fact, Othello's lack of this virtue could be the major theme of the play.

"FLOODING" AND BLURRED REALITY

In relationships, especially troubled ones, it can be hard to maintain that clear, prudent view of what is real and what is not. Dr. John Gottman, the noted marital therapist and researcher, tells us that when relationships become highly troubled, people become so embroiled in their problems that they enter into a state he calls "flooding." In the midst of a fight or other high-stress encounter, a person's heart races, blood pressure rises, and memory becomes impaired.

He or she cannot remember the full, positive range of events that occurred in their relationship. They often can only recall instances of negative experiences with their spouse or lover. Reality becomes distorted, partially as a mechanism that can be used to justify actions prudent people would not take. And according to copious research conducted by Gottman, persistent "flooding" is a predictor of violence and divorce.

We know that when the Othello response takes hold of a relationship and things "get crazy," reality is the first thing to go out the window:

- When Paula, a middle-aged executive, learned that her husband, Jim, was engaged in a flirtation with another woman (not yet an affair), she became incensed and convinced that Jim had been engaging in extramarital affairs for years and that he had been a "terrible husband." Even though Jim had not been behaving too virtuously lately, Jim had usually been a reliable and faithful husband. Perhaps Paula was painting Jim as all evil so she could then justify ending their marriage. We don't know. But we do know that for strong emotional reasons, Paula was failing to make decisions based on a good mental representation of reality. She was about to take emotional actions that were not fully in line with reality and, as a result, dire and long-lasting consequences were likely to result.

- When Constance decided to end her long-running relationship with her lover, Patricia, she told herself that Patricia had never been interesting enough or intelligent enough or caring enough to merit a long-running partnership. It had all been a mistake! For whatever reasons, Constance had decided to mentally turn away from all the good things about Patricia, the things that had attracted her to Patricia in the first place. Again, Constance was distorting reality for some reason, perhaps due to an inner urge to move out of the relationship. Like Paula above, she felt the need to construct an altered image of reality in order to justify some inner call to action.

■ When Carl, a college student, learned that his girlfriend, Samantha, wanted to end their relationship, he began to tell himself that she was a "slut." What other explanation could there be for her insanity? There had to be something wrong with her. He also told other people that she was a "slut." It was a terribly damaging charge to direct at Samantha, one that arose from his immature, wounded male pride and his anger and desire to damage someone whom he still liked and possibly loved. Later, when Samantha began to see someone else, he felt that his characterization of her had been proven. There it was, the proof that she was a promiscuous woman who was unworthy of him! Some men never get beyond such patterns. They stay rooted in an unvirtuous, reality-deficient world that they shape according to their own ego needs.

In order to get back in touch with reality and fight such "flooding," we usually need to find some mental stillness and create a "space" where we can think. In quiet solitude, we can often clarify the truth, what is real and what is not.

In that reflection, both Aristotle and Aquinas urge us to cultivate a virtue that is secondary to Prudence. It is known as the virtue of memoria.

The Virtue of Memoria

Memoria is a component of Prudence. It can be defined as the cultivation of memory that is true to reality. You might note that, in the case studies given just above, people have lost their sense of past truth. In the place of a true past, a false one has arisen to meet current needs and angry desires.

To build Memoria, we need to resist the human tendency to amplify and stew about wrongs that have been done to us. Instead, we need to take the higher path by seeking to identify and clarify the truth about the past by asking questions like these:

- "Do I have a balanced, realistic view of what has been both bad and good in my relationship, or am I now considering only the bad things? Do I remember the loving times, or am I now just mired in thinking about current problems and conflicts?"

- "Am I making something up, or is my view based on some true past reality that I can justify, prove, and show that actually happened?"

- "Is what I am thinking consistent with the history of our relationship, or is it out of line?"

- "Is there something in my own personal history—in my childhood, or in past relationships—that is shaping or coloring my current mood or impulses?"

Saint Thomas Aquinas, in particular, is adamant that we not dwell in current self-deceptions, but to strive to be true to real memory, to Memoria. He cites the great danger in creating a kind of false history, based on our current needs and frustrations.

By cultivating Memoria, we arrive at a balanced, realistic memory that results in a truer sense of what is taking place at the moment. There is another tool, too, that can be most helpful in promoting healthy consideration before we act. This is a virtue that both Aristotle and Saint Thomas Aquinas called facilitas.

IAGO AS FALSE COUNSELOR

In Shakespeare's play *Othello*, Iago can be taken as a representation of Facilitas—a good thing—that has gone terribly awry. Othello places his trust in an evil counselor, thereby opening himself, and his beloved, to untold harm and tragedy.

If there is a central moral admonition present in *Othello*, it is to doubt ourselves and our own perceptions above all. An important secondary point is to place our trust only in good counselors and even then to filter what they tell us through a considered, rich matrix of prudent consideration and thought.

FACILITAS

Facilitas, another component of Prudence, means seeking out good counsel from trustworthy people and then actually listening to what they have to say about our problems or the actions we are contemplating.

Practicing Facilitas means finding a friend or a counselor or a therapist whom you trust, whose judgment you respect. It means being honest and vulnerable enough to approach that person with your problem, in essence saying, "Here is the issue I am confronting, and here is what I think I might do about it."

Then it is time to sit back and listen to what they have

to say. All of us who have taken, or given, advice are keenly aware that there are risks. Often, we make mistakes like these:

- We gullibly take the advice of someone who has a personal or harmful agenda of their own. Perhaps, like Iago, they want to harm us. Or perhaps they want to experiment with our lives, or they have strong opinions on what represents "right" action, or they would like to see us do things that they lacked the courage to do when they were in similar circumstances themselves. In other words, they are giving false counsel, either intentionally or unintentionally.

- We seek advice from sycophantic friends who tell us that whatever action we are planning is wonderful, ideal—the very thing that needs to be done! In such cases, we are only

THE FAULTY COUNSELOR

Because she was experiencing marital friction, a woman named Mary called her old friend Carla and invited her to lunch. After all, Carla had been divorced and Mary needed a trusted friend to talk things over with her. Yet as soon as Mary said, "I wanted to talk to you about some problems we've been having at home," Carla jumped in and stated emphatically, "Call my lawyer! Call a divorce lawyer right now!"

Mary was smart enough to realize that Carla was eager to impose her own experience on her, and not really listening. In reality, Mary was still a long way from needing an attorney. She simply needed someone to listen to her and offer some ideas and advice.

This story points up a potential danger of Facilitas: the tendency to get sucked into the counselor's definition of your problem instead of keeping your own in sharp focus.

asking other people to rubber-stamp a decision we have already made, not seeking healthy perspective and feedback.

Instead, we need to speak with people who have demonstrated both wisdom and the ability to listen to us. Then we need the courage and integrity to actually listen to those good people, not to remain immovable about our views and the actions we are contemplating. In other words, we need to suspend our own plans and decisions, at least for the time we are engaged in Facilitas. We never need to slavishly do exactly what our chosen counselors tell us to do, but we do need to listen and process what they tell us. That is the point of engaging in Facilitas.

The ultimate goal is to arrive at a view that will prevent us from making imprudent actions. Imprudent actions, we know, only lead to further problems in the future. If we act brashly to cut off a love relationship, for example, we might find ourselves deeply regretting that decision later on. In life, it is often difficult to undo what we have done in the past.

There is yet another tool that is part of Prudence, one that does not have a Latin name: engaging in considered judgment and planning. It is often tempting, in a "flooding" state, to want to "show the other person" by acting quickly, brashly, and forcefully. Yet even when emotions are strong, part of Prudence is considering consequences before acting.

What are the risk factors in what we are planning to do? What are the potential consequences?

- If you go ahead and start to have an affair, what are the likely outcomes of that action? What foreseeable events are you about to unleash? Are you willing to accept them?

■ If you leave your spouse and home, what will the consequences be for yourself, your finances, your children, and so on? What will the impact be on you at work, in your community?

■ If you are acting purely out of anger, or to "show" a partner that you have the courage to do something brash, what will you have to do afterward to repair the damage, if that will even be possible?

The more careful the planning, the more you reduce risk factors. You equip yourself to avoid imprudent actions and move ahead both consciously and wisely.

THE PAYBACKS OF VIRTUOUS PRUDENCE

When we cultivate prudence, we begin to reap the benefits of a more considered, moderated life. These can play out in a variety of ways:

■ Frustrated by current frictions with your lover, you were thinking of ending your relationship. But striving to remember the many good things you had enjoyed in your relationship (in other words, the virtue Memoria) led you to take a more balanced approach. You decided to give your relationship more time and try to build upon its many good aspects.

■ You had a very negative view of your boyfriend, but listened to a trusted friend (in other words, you were practicing Facilitas by seeking wise counsel) who reopened your eyes to many positive traits your boyfriend actually possessed. The result was a new willingness to try to work things out and stay together.

THE ART OF PRUDENT ACTION

After you have engaged in careful considerations, action may no longer be desirable, or so immediately tempting. You have now framed the problem appropriately and gotten a better idea of the most virtuous actions to take.

However, there is another important component to Prudence, a quality of action that Aquinas calls Solertia. Solertia can be defined as the perfected ability to make quick decisions when unexpected events happen. Aquinas says, "In deliberation you may hesitate. But a considered act must be performed swiftly."

Yet Solertia, despite its speed, is based on healthy self-knowledge and a considered knowledge of the world. A person who has mastered Solertia might act in ways such as these:

- A woman on a business trip had a chance to engage in an anonymous sexual escapade with a man she met. Even though she had been experiencing frustrations in her marriage, she immediately rejected the idea without hesitation. In light of the potential consequences to her husband, her family, and herself, she could see at once that she was not going to allow her life to "go there."

- A divorced man had a parent/teacher conference with his son's third-grade teacher, a very attractive woman. When she took a tone that was flirtatious with him, he immediately took a step back and reestablished a professional tone. He immediately saw that he could only bring harm to his son, and conflict to himself, by adopting a philandering tone with this woman, who in her own turn was acting imprudently.

CULTIVATING SOLERTIA

Aristotle, Aquinas, and Peiper tell us that Solertia is usually not an innate trait in humans. We need to practice and cultivate it. Saint Thomas Aquinas, in particular, offers us some surprising advice on how Solertia can be cultivated:

- *We need to be physically fit.* This strikes contemporary people as a curious insight. What does being fit have to do with acting virtuously? Aquinas, however, says that in order to practice prudent Solertia, we need to be in fine tune, both cardiovascularly and neurologically. A certain level of fitness is needed if we are to be equipped to make sound judgments quickly. It is illuminating that Aquinas, who surely predated any and all of the current fitness "rages," knew that fitness and wellness functioned as important components in making the right decisions in our lives.

- *We need to live soberly and simply.* Drunkenness and slovenliness of all kinds immediately impede our abilities to practice Solertia. It is interesting how completely this factor has become ingrained in our popular culture. Consider Shakespeare's character Falstaff, for example, who can be seen as a living antithesis to Solertia. A fat drunk, his life is a constant pursuit of gluttony and lechery. His inexhaustible hunt for sexual escapades with pretty women leads him into folly and bad decisions until he finally becomes a public laughingstock.

Consider, too, the countless times that a lack of sobriety leads to sexual improprieties, both in real life and in fiction. Bars serving alcohol are traditional starting-places for sexual encounters. Cocktail parties function similarly. Back in the

1960s, Americans first learned of marijuana's efficacy in loosening people up for "love-ins" where indiscriminate sex was not held to be so blameworthy. And ever and always, fraternity parties with free-flowing beer are engineered to get young people drunk to the point where they lose the Solertia-like ability to make wise decisions about having sex with one another. Such examples point to the fact that sobriety is a key component of making wise, prudent decisions.

MEN'S AND WOMEN'S SEX FANTASIES

In a 1990 study, only 28 percent of American men reported having sexual fantasies involving partners with whom they were already involved. In contrast, 59 percent of women's fantasies included current partners.

Source: "Sex Differences in Sexual Fantasy: An Evolutionary Psychological Approach," by B. J. Ellis and D. Symons, *Journal of Sex Research*, vol. 27 (1990).

It might sound extremely old-fashioned to say that staying sober is part of being virtuous! But is it? With Virtue raised to the level of a classical virtue, it might not be such an outlandish observation after all.

RASHNESS: AN INEFFICIENT ALTERNATIVE TO SOLERTIA

The swiftness of Solertia should not be confused with rashness. Solertia is rapid action taken on a well-rounded, consistent knowledge of self and the world. Rashness, in contrast, is simply quick action. Quick, uncentered action is not only flawed; it is often destructive, causing us to do harm to both ourselves and others.

Rash actions can cause confusion and harm. Consider these examples:

- Jack suspected that his wife was having an affair, so he packed his bags and left her and their children behind. Later, when he realized the extent of his foolhardiness, he begged to be let back in.

- After a sexual encounter with a female colleague, a man named Emil announced to his wife of ten years that he was "in love with another woman." Not surprisingly, she asked him to move out. In a week, his relationship with the "other woman" was over. He begged his wife to let him come home and try to patch things up, but it was too late—he had done irreparable harm to his marriage.

- On the elevator in her office building after lunch one day, Suzanne was surprised when a male colleague of hers tried to kiss her. She was even more surprised when she and this man ended up necking heavily for a few minutes on the ride up to their floor. Afterward, Suzanne was embarrassed, chagrined, and at a loss to know how to proceed. She really didn't want it to happen, or at least, not in that way. It could have been prevented by a healthy level of Solertia on her part.

What is even worse than rashness? According to Saint Thomas Aquinas, it is something surprising: irresoluteness. There are many varieties. Some people know what they *should do*, but never act. Other people spend their lives looking at both sides of every question but stay stuck like the proverbial deer that freezes in the headlights of an oncoming car, unable to decide whether to move to the left or the right.

CHAPTER 19
LIVING A TEMPERATE LIFE

Let me not to the marriage of true minds
Admit impediments. Love is not love
Which alters when it alteration finds,
Or bends with the remover to remove:
O, no! it is an ever-fixed mark,
That looks on tempests and is never shaken;
It is the star to every wandering bark,
Whose worth's unknown, although his height be taken.
Love's not Time's fool, though rosy lips and cheeks
Within his bending sickle's compass come;
Love alters not with his brief hours and weeks,
But bears it out even to the edge of doom.
If this be error and upon me proved,
I never writ, nor no man ever loved.

—Shakespeare, Sonnet #116

TEMPERANCE, LIKE PRUDENCE, IS another of the classical cardinal Virtues—and another that can become a powerful, life-orienting force that offers insulation against jealousy and the Othello response. Like Prudence, *Temperance* is a word that has taken on a new set of connotations and meanings in contemporary life. It has come to mean moderation, lack of passion, and sobriety.

The classical view of Temperance is far broader in scope, actually not devoid of passion. Saint Thomas Aquinas defines Temperance as serenity of spirit.

To understand this virtue more completely, think of the *tempering* of a blank piece of steel that will become the blade of a sword. In ancient times, such blades were tempered by being heated repeatedly, hammered to harden them, then plunged into cold water. Then the process was repeated many times.

Through hard work and intelligent development, something unfinished became able to serve a function in the world. In the process, it had even become beautiful — or in any case, as beautiful as a weapon could become.

Similarly, temperance is achieved by achieving order in yourself, by reorienting yourself and taking care of yourself in such a way that you can be true to your life and, by extension, true to those whom you love.

As was the case with Prudence, Temperance can be broken down into several components.

CASSIO AND RODERIGO: OUR SHADOW SELVES

Cassio and Roderigo, two supporting characters in Othello, shed their own light on the Othello response.

Cassio is an honest, true, and steady man. Unfortunately for him, Othello promoted him instead of Iago. It was the event that launched Iago's demoniacal plot against Othello and then Desdemona.

Roderigo, the opposite of Cassio, is a dull-witted, lumbering henchman ready to do Iago's dirty work where Iago himself cannot engage in visible evildoing. Early in the play, Iago can get Cassio drunk, but he cannot be the person to pick a sword fight with him. To do so would have caused Iago to be discredited in Othello's eyes, ending the plot before it began. At the end of the play, Roderigo ambushes and stabs Cassio while Iago remains unseen.

Yet aren't Cassio and Roderigo, different as they are, the same man. They both serve as shadow selves to Othello, the greater man upon whom their destinies hang. Roderigo shows us a base, unimaginative, and gullible man—a representation of the part of ourselves that emerges when we succumb to obsessive jealousy. Cassio shows us the opposite—the path of honesty and good we can choose in our lives. His is the kind of life that is resistant to the Othello response.

Othello might have chosen either path—the higher road of Cassio or the base road of Roderigo. When we are confronted with the "green monster" of jealousy, we can make a similar choice—to be either a Cassio or a Roderigo in our lives.

THE FIRST KEY TO TEMPERANCE: BUILD YOUR LIFE ON TRUE REALITY

In his writings, Saint Thomas Aquinas told us that Temperance can be achieved only when we cultivate an ability to act that is based on a realistic, true perspective about what is happening, and has happened, in the world. In contemporary context, this admonition becomes clear. When we act based on a worldview that we have allowed to become distorted due to our ego needs—insecurities, anger, and distrust—we are incapable of acting well. We need to step back and make sure we take action based not on what we *think* is happening (or what we fear or hope for), but on an objective assessment of reality.

Clearly, the ability to cultivate this virtue has a great deal to do with our level of success in love relationships. After all, many of the real-world events that arise in the wake of the Othello response (the stalkings, confrontations, leave-takings, and the rest) are the direct outcomes of unrealistic beliefs that are justified through unrealistic views of what has taken place in the real world.

What are the keys to building this heightened level of reality awareness, which leads to Temperance? We need to be asking ourselves some probing, self-assessing questions:

- *Are you taking good care of yourself?* This seems like an odd question until we stop to consider how much harm we do ourselves by acting intemperately. When we are afflicted with the Othello response, we are actively trying to destroy not only those around us, but ourselves and those we love too. At the very least, we are trying to inflict terrible emotional damage upon ourselves. It is as though we have unleashed our personal Iago and allowed him to destroy our lives. A temperate outlook, in contrast, leads us to take time to cultivate a certain kindness toward ourselves and those we love. Curiously, such self-care usually leads us to a better conception of reality.

- *Where are you in danger (emotional, and even physical) in your life, and why?* This unusual question, again, can help uncover areas where our conception of reality is off base or distorted by our internal distortions and insecurities. If you feel in danger of harming yourself or a loved one because of your jealousy, for example, that is valuable information you need to know if you are determined to direct your life toward a higher, more virtuous path.

- *Are you out of touch with all that is best in you?* Gentleness, openness, honesty, and other positive traits most of us possessed in our early years can be driven away in adult life by the distortions of jealousy. Viewed in this way, our half-forgotten youthful virtues stand as a call back to the right, virtuous path.

■ *What kind of physical shape are you in?* Yes, being in good shape is a key to Temperance too. Aristotle, very early on, told us that it is very difficult to make good life assessments if we are not in good physical condition.

■ *What is your current mental state?* What's keeping you sharp in terms of your own mental processes? Are you being challenged in some way that's positive, or are you being torn down by negative thinking, jealousy, or blame?

■ *How are you doing spiritually?* Is there a sense of gratitude in your life? Is there a generosity of spirit in your relationship, in your marriage, in your family? Are you willing to make sacrifices that make a difference in other people's lives? Are you exercising compassion? If you can answer yes to such questions, you are closer to a positive reality.

■ *What are you avoiding?* Are you avoiding the process of mending your marriage, growing closer to your children, or something else? The things we are putting off can help us get a wider view of the reality we have created for ourselves, which might not be a true one. What are some dreams that you had that you set aside? Maybe you need to take them on. Maybe you need to be aggressive in taking on a new creative project. Whatever it is you need to claim for yourself in terms of creativity, maybe you need to challenge yourself in some new way in order to get your larger life centered and back on track.

A Second Key to Temperance: Cultivate an Observing Ego

"Observing ego" is not an ancient term. It is one that has been coined by modern psychotherapists. Observing ego, in essence, means a keen ability to see yourself.

Having an observing ego means that you have cultivated the ability to observe yourself and to calmly assess what you're doing in all areas of your life. It takes work, but the process can be aided by keeping a journal, talking to your partner about how you're feeling, what you're doing, what's going on inside you, and sharing your dreams.

Another help in building an observing ego is to actively cultivate the habit of responding instead of reacting. ("Respond, don't react" is a Buddhist saying.) Very often when somebody says something to us that's provocative, we retaliate in kind or we become immediately defensive.

"Respond, don't react" means that we should slow down, think through what is happening, and respond appropriately: usually with compassion and a degree of self-control that are appropriate to the true reality of the situation. It is similar to Aquinas's notion of Solertia, which means making the right decision quickly, and in a very considered way, based on reality.

A Third Key to Temperance: Slow Down

Slowing down interaction with our partners gives us more opportunities and choices to say the right thing, or to see the true reality of the situation rather than jumping into automatic responses that are often defensive or critical. Slowing down allows us to arrive at a more considered response to what's happening in our lives.

Slowing down can mean any of the following things, and more:

- When your partner criticizes you, you take a quick deep breath and calm yourself before answering.

- Strive to think and speak the truth. We all know how difficult that can be when we are confronted with unpleasant events, accusations, or tendencies.

- When you are contemplating taking some important action that will have a major impact on your relationship (to ask your husband for a trial separation, to break off a relationship, to begin a new relationship or even an affair), take a day or even an afternoon to consciously slow the pace of your thinking and approach the action from a place of calm and consideration.

- Before saying something critical of your spouse or partner, slow your temptation to lash out with something unkind. By pulling away from a tendency to attack or criticize, you bring a new timing and consciousness to your relationship that can let you act in ways that are more in line with both kindness and reality.

We live in a time of convenience, when taking the right medication or reading the right book promises to provide an instant quantum leap in the quality of our lives. The process of cultivating the virtue of Temperance, in contrast, comes from an earlier time, when we were expected to work long and hard to create a better life for ourselves—a life based on a perfected understanding of both self and the world around us.

The rewards of all that work? A higher state of being. We are less prone to act in ways that cause damage, less likely to hurt ourselves and others unnecessarily, and better able to recover and heal from life's calamitous events. As Pieper wrote, "The fruits of Temperance are a mature manliness [and womanliness, of course—the authors] and a certain beauty." This cultivated, virtuous beauty can help us remain grounded in true reality and insulate us surely against incursions of the Othello response.

In the end, may we learn to live and love with wisdom and kindness. Let that stand as the hope we hold for you, the readers of this book.

RESOURCES

BOOKS

- *Out of the Shadows: Understanding Sexual Addiction* by Patrick J. Carnes (Hazelden Books). An excellent resource for those with sexual addiction and impulse control issues. Dr. Carnes's other books on other sexual addictions, including addiction to Internet sex, are worth exploring if you are seeking focused advice for specific sexual compulsions.

- *Why Marriages Succeed or Fail: And How You Can Make Yours Last* by John Gottman (Three Rivers Press). The best research-based book on marital health. Gottman is the top researcher on what makes for happy, healthy marriages. We recommend his other books as well.

ORGANIZATIONS AND INSTITUTIONS

- Alanon Support Groups (www.al-anon.alateen.org). You need not be married to an alcoholic to join an Alanon group. They offer powerful help in getting you to detach with love and not get pulled into dangerous, reactive behaviors such as the Othello response.

- The Meadows in Wickenburg, Arizona, is a clinic specializing in treatment for addictive sexual and other disorders. Dr. Patrick J. Carnes (see book listing above) is on staff. For information on their programs, call (928) 684-4001.

INTERNET RESOURCES

- Alanon support groups (www.al-anon.alateen.org; see comments above).

- Othello Response Website (www.othelloresponse.com). This is the website that the authors of *The Othello Response* have created to promote awareness of the Othello response and provide rapid referrals and other help to sufferers.

- Therapist Locator Net (www.therapistlocator.net). A great resource for finding a qualified marriage/relationship therapist who can help change and improve your relationship. It is the website for the American Association of Marriage and Family Therapists, representing over six thousand therapists across the country.

ACKNOWLEDGMENTS

WE THANK OUR FAMILIES for their support and encouragement while we researched and wrote this book. Both Susan Harriss (Dr. Kenneth Ruge's wife) and Fran Taber (Barry Lenson's wife) provided a steady stream of good ideas and sound advice at every stage of the project.

We would also like to thank the many people whose stories became case studies in this book. We know some of you firsthand. Others we know from reading about you in the news or other sources. It is our hope that your stories will help our readers deal more effectively with the Othello response.

We thank Matthew Lore, our editor and publisher at Marlowe & Company, for entrusting this important project to us. It was Matthew who first called our attention to the problem of obsessive jealousy and suggested this book's name. Without Matthew, this volume would not exist.

We also thank our agent, Gareth Esersky at the Carol Mann Agency, for all she did for this project. She is our agent and also a wise counselor and friend. A rare combination, indeed.

Last and certainly too late, we thank William Shakespeare for writing *Othello*, the play that delineated the devastations of the Othello response with harrowing accuracy and perceptiveness. One reason such geniuses are put on this earth is to provide ordinary people with the wisdom we need to live happily and wisely.

ABOUT THE AUTHORS

Dr. KENNETH C. RUGE and BARRY LENSON frequently write together about health, psychological well-being, and relationships.

Dr. Kenneth C. Ruge is a marriage and family therapist who practices in New York City. For over twenty-five years he has been working with couples going through the Othello response and other issues, helping them to heal and redesign their marriages. A contributor to the *Ladies' Home Journal* column, "Can This Marriage be Saved?" Dr. Ruge is a frequent lecturer on marital health and parenting issues. He is the author of *Where Do I Go From Here?* and coauthor, with Nina Frost and Richard Shoup, of *Soul Mapping: An Imaginative Way to Self-Discovery.*

Barry Lenson lives in Millburn, New Jersey. He is author of *Good Stress, Bad Stress* and coauthor of *Simple Steps* (with Dr. Arthur Caliandro), *Lost and Found* (with Dr. Arthur Caliandro), *Take Control of Your Life* (with Dr. Richard Shoup), *Multicultural and Ethnic Marketing* (with Alfred L. Schreiber), and other books. Also an active journalist, Mr. Lenson has been editor in chief of *The Organized Executive, Working Smart, Executive Strategies,* and *The New York Opera Newsletter.* His articles have appeared in *National Business Employment Weekly, The Wall Street Journal Interactive Edition, Yahoo! Internet Life,* and *Chamber Music Magazine* and other publications.

Both Dr. Ruge and Mr. Lenson can be contacted via the Othello response website, www.othelloresponse.com.